WHAT HAPPENS WHEN WE DIE?

To Heaven When I Die?

The few remaining Bible prophecies are rapidly coming to fruition. Begin studying your Bible without delay.

Truth For Today
P.O. Box 4
Littlethorpe
Leicester
www.tftuk@aol.com

This book is dedicated to Sister RennieAnn Lindsay of the Homeward Bound Fellowship, she has inspired and encouraged me to write this book

PROLOGUE

You may have experienced the following scenario: Often, at a funeral, the pastor may try to soothe the congregation by saying, "Don't worry, Albert is in Heaven, looking down on us". Later, at the graveyard, the same preacher says, "Don't worry Albert is resting in the grave, awaiting the resurrection at the return of Jesus". Pastor, which one is it?

Is a dead person taken to Heaven as soon as they die, or are they buried and await the resurrection when Jesus returns? Readers, there should be no confusion. Allow the Bible to answer this question: *"In a moment, in the twinkling of an eye, at the final trump: for the trumpet shall sound, and the dead shall be raised incorruptible, and we shall be changed."* For this *corruptible must put on incorruption, and this mortal must put on immortality"* (1 Corinthians 15:52–53). As you can see, the dead will be revived with the sound of the final trumpet, which signals Jesus' return, and not before that moment.

The scriptures also reveals that when Jesus returns, we will be transformed from mortal to immortal creatures. Right now, we are all mortal, exposed to pain and the prospect of death. In truth, only God possesses immortality. The blessed and sole Potentate, the King of Kings and Lord of Lords, is the only one who has immortality. If we went directly to Heaven, Hell, or Purgatory when we died, we would be immortal, but this is not the case. The doctrine of an immortal soul is just not biblical. The word soul appears more than 1600 times in the Bible, although it is never referred to as immortal. The idea of an immortal soul has its roots in ancient pagan religions and New Age philosophies.

CHAPTER 1: THE DEAD KNOW NOTHING

Why Do We die?

In Genesis 3, we learn that Eve was duped into eating from the Tree of Knowledge of Good and Evil, and she shared some of the fruit with her husband, Adam, who also ate it. God had told Adam and Eve that they could eat from any tree in the garden except one, and if they ate from the Tree of Knowledge of Good and Evil, they would die. According to the Bible, the wages of sin are death.

Sin initially appeared in the Garden of Eden, at the beginning of time. Because of our sinful natures, we shall all face physical death at some point. *"For the wages of sin is death; but the gift of God is eternal life through Jesus Christ, our Lord."* (Rom. 6:23). The consequence for sin is death, and only God possesses the power and authority to grant eternal life to His redeemed. Until that time, death remains an unconscious state for all humans. When Christ, our Saviour, appears, both the risen and the living righteous will be glorified and 'taken up' to meet their Lord.

Man was formed in the image of God, yet he did not inherit all of God's characteristics. God is both almighty and omniscient. In fact, despite being made in God's image, man lacks these characteristics and was never intended to have them. Humans were formed in God's image, both in look and character. (See Exodus 33:22, 23; Ezek 1:26-28; Genesis 5:1; James 3:9). Our first parents experienced a life free of degradation and death until they chose to sin (Romans 5:12-19; 1 Corinthians 15:21).

The terms "immortal" or "immortality" are never used in Scripture to refer to humanity's earthly, fallen existence. Every Christian believer is assured that Christ will give eternal life to those who persistently seek glory, honour, and immortality (Rom. 2:7). They do not yet have immortality, but they are looking forward to it. Immortality at the second coming (1 Cor. 15:51-54) is achievable because Christ purchased it for us at Calvary (2 Tim. 1:10). God is the only one who is immortal in comparison to terrestrial humans (1 Tim. 6:16).

The Soul And Spirit

Christianity has taken a mostly secular perspective on the two words' soul and spirit' in terms of their meaning and ultimate implications. Most people use these terms interchangeably, and they assume they are referring to some aspect of our spiritual nature, an immaterial being that continues to exist even after the body dies. However, as we continue to study the Bible and examine these words in greater detail in terms of what the Bible says about them, we will discover that the Bible paints a totally different picture. Let us begin with Genesis 2:7: *"And the Lord God formed man from the dust of the ground and breathed into his nostrils the breath of life; and man became a living soul."* What we see here are the fundamental building blocks of how God describes how he created man. God also describes how the body was fashioned from the dust of the ground, and how God breathed the breath into man, transforming him into a living soul. So it does not imply that God created a soul for man, but rather that man became a soul. When the body and bread of life, or the life-giving energy that God supplies to each of us, join together, we all become 'living souls'. It may be argued that we do not have a soul but rather that we are souls, and when we die, we become dead souls.

Now that we've established that the soul, at least in Biblical terms, does not refer to a living and thinking spiritual entity that lives on after the body dies, let's look at this intriguing word, "spirit." To do so, we'll go to Psalms 104:29, which states, *"Thou hidest thy face, they are troubled: thou takest away their breath, they die, and return to their dust."* This verse reverses the sequence of what we just saw in Genesis. We have the body reverting to dust as soon as God takes away our breath of life, which makes perfect sense because if that breath of life is the energy that God bestows on us, transforming us into flesh and blood, then our bodies should perish when the Creator returns that living energy, that life force. At this point, we simply revert to the state we were in before God joined the body and breath. We succumb to death. The most notable component is the Hebrew word for breath, 'Ruach'. Ruach, as used here, literally means wind, gust, ejection, or breath. As a result, we conclude that it is describing a vital force that provides breath to a living creature. This word can relate to a person's emotional condition in a variety of contexts, including the verse "a spirit of heaviness." That spirit of heaviness represents a spirit of despair when a person has been sad, yet we see in this verse from this passage a clear connection to the breath of life, the same breath that God gave when he created man as a living soul at the beginning.

Now that we know what Psalm 104:29 implies, let's look at the term 'ruach' in Ecclesiastes 12:7. Here, we find a very similar text that would eventually describe the exact process that we have just witnessed. However, this passage can be misleading since we have a preconceived sense that the spirit is a living and thinking being that lives on after the body dies, leading us to the wrong conclusion. Let's look at this verse and see what it declares: *"Then shall the dust return to the surface of the earth as it was, and the spirit shall return unto God who gave it."* As has been said, many people believe that this is the spirit being, the spiritual part of us that never truly dies, and that when the body dies, it separates and goes to God in heaven, which is the generally held belief. On the contrary, what many people are unfamiliar with is that the word there for spirit is the same word that was used earlier in Psalms for the term breath, 'ruach', which implies breath on exhale. It refers to the breath of life that God gave us in the beginning. This is a reinforcement of the idea that the body returns to dust and the breath of life, or spirit, returns to the God who fashioned it. The word returns' additionally becomes significant in this particular setting. Something can only return to its original location. In other words, for the spirit to return to God, it required a descent from him. If we properly define the term 'ruach,' we can see that what we're dealing with here is simply the return of the breath that brings life to God, and when that occurs, the body dies and man becomes a dead soul. It's fascinating to consider that from Genesis to Revelation, there is absolutely no mention of the soul or spirit as a living and thinking being worthy of existing independently of the body. It is only ever expressed as that breath of life, that life force from God, in the context of the spirit; when it comes to the soul, we read in the Bible that we are souls, but we do not possess souls.

"The Souls Of Dead Martyrs Crying Out For Vindication"?

First, it should be noted that the book of Revelation contains an abundance of prophetic symbolism. No one would want to believe that the four living creatures, the 24 elders, or the Lamb of chapters 4 and 5 appear exactly as John saw them in a vision. God revealed to John an ordered series of symbolic visions that we can correctly interpret by comparing Scripture to Scripture.

Second, if we look at the 'souls under the altar' in Revelation 6:9 literally, we get a strange picture. Why are they gathering under the altar in heaven? Their situation does not appear to be particularly comfortable; they appear to be disgruntled persons in desperate need of vindication.

Third, why should these martyrs be pleading with God to "avenge" the injustice done to them if their cruel foes went to hell after death, as immortal-soul believers believe? If the wicked's immortal souls go to hell when they die, vengeance must already be poured out on those who murdered the martyrs.

Fourth, it is critical to realise that the 'altar' in Revelation 6:9 is not the altar of incense in heaven. It alludes to the burnt sacrifice altar in the court of the ancient Israelite sanctuary or temple (Exodus 27:1–8; 29:12–18; 38:1–7). We can be certain of this because John's vision featured people who had been sacrificed. The only available place for Israelites to offer sacrifices was beside the altar of burnt offerings in the sanctuary's court (Lev. 17:1–9). The additional blood that was collected from animal sacrifices was poured at the base of the altar of the burned offering (Lev. 4:7, 18, 25, 30). According to Genesis 9:4, Deuteronomy 12:23, and Leviticus 17:10–11, the blood contained the animal's life (Hebrew nephesh or Greek psuche, meaning "life" or "soul"). When the animal's blood was poured beneath the altar, it symbolised life being poured out: Christ's life poured out for us (Heb. 10:1–9; Ps. 22:14), as well as the lives of Christ's people sacrificed for Him (2 Cor. 1:5; Phil. 3:10; Heb. 11:37).

The Hebrew and Greek words for "soul" (nephesh and psuche) do not refer to a separate part of the body, but rather to individuals who gave their blood for Christ's sake. These "souls" or "lives" were yelling out to God from the earth in a metaphorical sense, much like Abel's blood cried out for justice (Gen. 4:10).

The message of Revelation 6:9-11 is a wonderful reminder of God's ongoing compassion for those who have given their lives for Him. He has a record of their injustice, which begs to be vindicated, and they are deemed worthy in heaven and instructed to "rest yet for a little season" (verse 11). When Jesus returns, they will be woken from their death sleep and given their eternal inheritance (1 Thessalonians 4:13-18).

What Happens When We Die?

As I previously stated in this piece, the dead have no awareness at all; they know nothing, feel nothing, and remember nothing. People who die do not go to heaven or hell, but instead continue to live in consciousness. They go to the grave, where their bodies decay because the 'life essence' has been eradicated. They are sleeping, unconcerned about what is happening on Earth or in Heaven. The Bible clearly states that the righteous dead are not in heaven and the wicked dead are not in a realm of fire. They are in the dust of the earth, waiting for the resurrection day. That day for the righteous will be Christ's second arrival. The wicked will be called to account at the end of the millennium and put into eternal sleep.

The purpose of this article is to examine Bible passages that are used as evidence by people who believe in the immortality of the soul. It will be demonstrated that the true meaning of each passage in its scriptural context rules out the idea that the soul is eternal. According to the Bible, those who have died are no longer aware of time or what is happening on Earth. Death is like a deep sleep in which the body rests and the breath of life that sustains the body and soul returns to God until the resurrection. Whether you've lost a loved one or are interested about what happens after death, everyone asks this topic at some point.

Here are some verses that clearly state what happens when we die:

- Ecclesiastes 9:5-6: *"For the living know that they shall die: but the dead know not any thing, neither have they any more a reward; for the memory of them is forgotten. Also their love, and their hatred, and their envy, is now perished; neither have they any more a portion for ever in any thing that is done under the sun"* .

- Psalm 146:4 reads: *"His breath goeth forth, he returneth to his earth; in that very day his thoughts perish"*

- Psalm 6, verse 5, *"For in death there is no remembrance of thee: in the grave who shall give thee thanks"* ?
- Psalm 115:17, *"The dead praise not the Lord, neither any that go down into silence".*

When we examine these four passages and summarise the key points, we see that the dead know nothing, have no emotions, no thoughts, no connection to anything under the sun, no recollection of God, and do not praise the Lord; rather, the Bible describes the dead as having entered a state of silence. This begs the question: if we die, will we go straight to paradise or hell? Would this be our experience, or should we expect to dream about and experience new and extraordinary adventures, especially for those who go to heaven? Surely those who enter paradise will find delight, memory of God, and praise in him? In contrast, this is not the experience portrayed in the Bible; instead, there will be silence. The Bible states that it will be as if we are sleeping. This reference to death as a form of slumber is mentioned throughout the Old Testament.

In 1 Kings 11:43, it says, *"And Solomon died with his fathers and was buried in the city of David his father, and Rehoboam his son reigned in his place."* This verse in scripture is fairly typical of what we would see in the Old Testament. There is a persistent reference to a dead person going to sleep and being buried, sometimes alongside their fathers, which is a recurring subject. In fact, more than fifty passages refer to death as a type of sleep.

Another crucial line from the book of Job paints a vivid picture of our experience with death. Keep in mind that Moses wrote the book of Job after walking with God and experiencing a face-to-face contact with him. Moses spent 40 days with God, learning from him and receiving the law, as well as instructions to teach Israel the truth about God and our everlasting truths through the Gospel message. Moses gives an account about the experience we would have in death, in Job 14:10-14, *"But man dieth, and wasteth away: yea, man giveth up the ghost, and where is he? As the waters fail from the sea, and the flood decayeth and drieth up: So man lieth down, and riseth not: till the heavens be no more, they shall not awake, nor be raised out of their sleep.O that thou wouldest hide me in the grave, that thou wouldest keep me secret, until thy wrath be past, that thou wouldest appoint me a set time, and remember me! If a man die, shall he live again? all the days of my appointed time will I wait, till my change come."* This illustrates that in death, there is no remembrance of God. Moses says that we will go down into stillness, that we will not be woken, that we will not rise from our graves, but that God has set an appointed moment for him to remember us, and that at this point, as Job predicts, change will occur. That shift will come with the second coming of Christ, when this mortal coil will take on immortality, and the dead will be risen first.

When it comes to the status of the dead, different religions and groups have different beliefs about what happens after death. For instance, an oil lamp requires both a wick and oil to produce light, and the body needs God's breath to function. Some people believe in purgatory, reincarnation, the soul's immortality, the afterlife, and so on.

CHAPTER 2: NEW TESTAMENT

What Did Jesus Say About Death?

Jesus stated: *"And fear not them which kill the body, but are not able to kill the soul: but rather fear him which is able to destroy both soul and body in hell."* (Matt. 10:28, emphasis added). Advocates of immortal souls use this passage to emphasise the contrast between soul and body, saying that the soul is the true self that resides within the body during life but separates from it after death. The difficulty with this viewpoint is that this scripture demonstrates that the soul, like the body, can be annihilated in hell. If the soul can be destroyed, it is not immortal and will not suffer forever in hellfire. The text's message is that, although

Matthew 10:28 uses the Greek word for "soul" (psuche), which implies "life." The identical term appears four times in Matthew 16:25 and 26; in the King James Version Bible, it is translated as "life" in verse 25 and "soul" in verse 26. *"For whoever saves his life [psuche] will lose it, and whoever loses his life [psuche] for my sake will find it."* What good is it for a man to gain the whole world but lose his own soul? *"What shall a man give in exchange for his soul [psuche]?"* Notice how the translators utilised several translations of the same Greek phrase. Verse 25 says that one may lose his soul for Christ's cause. This would be impossible if the soul were an immortal being within man. For those who believe in the immortal soul, losing one's soul means going to hell. Obviously, no one goes to hell for Jesus' sake. It is possible, however, to lay down one's life for Christ's cause. The translators, who believed in the immortality of the soul, recognised the difficulty and translated the word "psuche" as "life," despite the fact that it was translated as "soul" in verse 26.

The true meaning of Matthew 16:25-26 is that anyone who prioritises selfish desires over Christ's ministry will lose eternal life. Those who love and serve Christ, however, will get eternal life. The following passage provides context for the statement: *"For the Son of man shall come in the glory of his Father with his angels; and then he shall reward every man according to his works"* (verse 27). In Matthew 10:28, Jesus states that the unbeliever's "soul" or "life" will be destroyed forever, which is completely consistent with Jesus' teaching that the unbeliever's "soul" or "life" will be destroyed forever. The phrase "everlasting punishment" refers to the eternal loss of life, not the endless life of loss.

In John 5:28-29, Jesus tells the Jews about the state of the dead: *"Marvel not at this: for the hour is coming, in which all that are in the graves shall hear his voice, And shall come forth; they that have done good, unto the resurrection of life; and they that have done evil, unto the resurrection of damnation"* (John 5:28-29). Jesus describes the dead as staying in their graves, awaiting resurrection, either to life or to condemnation. According to the prophet Daniel, *"And many of them that sleep in the dust of the earth shall awake, some to everlasting life, and some to shame and everlasting contempt"*. Daniel 12:2. This scripture demonstrates that our destinies do not begin when we die, but at the resurrection.

In Acts 2:29, 34, we read, *"Men and brethren, let me freely speak unto you of the patriarch David, that he is both dead and buried, and his sepulchre is with us unto this day. For David is not ascended into the heavens: but he saith himself, The Lord said unto my Lord, Sit thou on my right hand."* If there is anyone we expect to be in heaven, it's David. Many of the Bible's heroes, including David, are not in heaven. In the New Testament, we read in Acts 2:29, 34, *"Men and brethren, let me freely speak unto you of the patriarch David, that he is both dead and buried, and his sepulchre is still with us today."* For David has not gone into the heavens; rather, he says, *"The Lord said to my Lord, Sit on my right hand."* If there is anyone we anticipate to see in heaven, it is David. While he was not perfect, he was regarded as a man who was constantly seeking God, and his Psalms are filled with yearning and praise for the Lord (1 Sam 13:14). However, we are told that David has yet to reach paradise.

Throughout his life on earth, Jesus demonstrated that death was not permanent and that he had a plan to defeat it. He demonstrated God's power over death via his own resurrection and promised that one day he will return to defeat death once and for all. He detailed how things would be at the End Times, and how we'd all have to choose between following him or going our own way, accepting eternal life with Him or losing it forever. Finally, He vowed that one day He would make everything right, resurrect those who had died, and transport us all to heaven. John, the disciple, wrote: *"And I heard a great voice out of heaven saying, Behold, the tabernacle of God is with men, and he will dwell with them, and they shall be his people, and God himself shall be with them, and be their God."And God will wipe away every tear from their eyes, and there will be no more death, sorrow, crying, or pain, for the old things have passed away."* (Revelation 21:3–4).

There is a misconception that we are now in the New Testament and that because Jesus died for our sins and resurrected from the dead, we will go directly to Heaven when we die. Here we will examine whether or not the New Testament agrees with the Old Testament. We'll begin with some verses on what Jesus said, then go on to Paul's writings and how they all fit together. First, we'll look at Luke 8:52-53, *"And all wept and bewailed her; but he said, Weep not; she is not dead, but sleeps."They mocked him, knowing she was dead."* A young girl has died, and when Jesus appears, the parents are in mourning. The main points of Jesus' statement are:

• Jesus refers to death as a sleep, which is quite consistent with what we have read in the Old Testament.

• God sees death differently.

While we regard death as a finality or end point, God regards it as a type of sleep, which is significant because we shall later discuss the distinction between the 'first death' and the 'second death'. Hopefully, we can establish that everyone who dies enters a sleep-like state while awaiting the resurrection.

Let's look at some more evidence by returning to John's account of Lazarus, who also died and was previously mentioned by Jesus in a similar way. John 11:11 to 14: *"These things said he: and after that he said to them, Our friend Lazarus sleepeth; but I go, that I may awaken him out of sleep"* The disciples said, *"Lord, if he sleeps, he will do well"*. Although Jesus mentioned death, some took it as a reference to sleep. Jesus informed them that "Lazarus has died." Again, there is no misunderstanding when Jesus appears and declares that death is a sleep. The disciples are perplexed by the terminology, believing Jesus is referring to Lazarus as having fallen asleep when, in fact, He is speaking clearly about Lazarus' death. Once again, Jesus affirms his opinion that death is a state of sleep. He did not indicate that Lazarus was looking down from Heaven, but rather that he was asleep in the grave. Again, Jesus' remarks are widely misconstrued, therefore we will seek more credible proof.

Let us dig deeper into the New Testament, about twenty years after Jesus' death and resurrection, to the time of Paul's writings. In 1 Corinthians 15:17-18, Paul alludes to death as a sleep, saying, *"And if Christ is not raised, your faith is futile; you are still in your sins."* Then those who have fallen asleep in Christ perish," and 1 Corinthians 15:51, *"Behold, I show you a mystery: We shall not all sleep, but we shall all be changed."* Once again, Paul describes death as a nap. He refuses to modify his mind and discuss death, claiming that there is no such thing as death and that we all go straight to heaven. In the Old Testament, Paul, Jesus, and Moses remain in complete harmony. All of the Apostles discuss death in the same way.

Long ago, people had a totally different perspective on mortality than we do today. Whereas many people today believe that when we die, we go straight to heaven, they used to believe that dying was the end of everything, that they died, and that there was no prospect of eternal life in heaven or on Earth. In dealing with that mentality, Paul wrote to the Thessalonian

Church (1 Thessalonians 4:15-16), *"For this we say unto you by the word of the Lord, that we which are alive and remain unto the coming of the Lord shall not prevent them which are asleep. For the Lord himself shall descend from heaven with a shout, with the voice of the archangel, and with the trump of God: and the dead in Christ shall rise first:".* Examining Paul's letter, we can conclude that if the dead had died and gone to Heaven, Paul would have simply remarked, *"Do not worry about the dead because they are in Heaven watching over us."* However, Paul does not do this; instead, he informs the crowd that in the future, the dead will be raised and we will all be given new bodies, after which we will meet the Lord in the air.

According to Acts 2:34, David did not ascend to heaven. We know that David was a man after God's own heart, so he would almost certainly be in Heaven. The only reason he isn't there yet is that the Second Advent hasn't happened. The above scripture clearly shows that when we die, we enter a state of sleep, in which we have no conscious consciousness until Christ returns.

The Lord often gives prophets visions and dreams that make them appear to be far away from their earthly home. However, this does not prove that humans have an eternal soul. The Apostle Paul, for example, experienced visions and revelations from the Lord.

First, we should recognise that Paul was talking about himself. He was discussing how God had given him "visions and revelations" (verse 1; compare verses 6-11). His goal was to persuade the Corinthians that he was a truly inspired apostle (verses 11-12). In his vision, Paul was transported to paradise (verse 4), the third heaven (verse 2). Paradise contains God's throne and the tree of life (Revelation 2:7; 22:1, 2). Paul wasn't sure if he was in bodily form in heaven or just in a vision while his body remained on earth. The point is that Paul was still a human being living on Earth when God revealed to him visions and insights. He wasn't a disembodied ghost whose body had died and his spirit now lives in heaven. The paragraph contains no evidence to support the immortality of the soul.

"God Is Not The God Of The Dead, But Of The Living"

Jesus told the Sadducees, *"For in the resurrection, they neither marry nor are given in marriage, but are like the angels of God in heaven. But, as for the resurrection of the dead, have you not read what God spoke to you, stating, I am the God of Abraham, Isaac, and Jacob? God is not the God of the dead, but of the living"* (Matthew 22:30-32). This phrase, is a conversation between Jesus and the Sadducees about the resurrection. The Sadducees doubted that the dead would be resurrected (verse 23). They presented a hypothetical scenario in which a woman married seven brothers in succession and asked Jesus which of the brothers would be her spouse after the resurrection. Jesus' response focused on the resurrection: *"For in the resurrection they neither marry, nor are given in marriage "And as touching the dead, that they rise:... God is not the God of the dead, but of the living"* (verses 31, 32). Jesus' point was that God is the God of the living because the dead will be raised in the resurrection, not because the dead are already living in spirit form in heaven. ..In Mark 12:26, Luke cites Jesus as saying, *"And the fact that the dead are raised."* Moses also reveals this in the burning bush story, referring to the Lord as the God of Abraham, Isaac, and Jacob.

Now he is the God of the living, not the dead (Luke 20:37–38). The final sentence of Luke 20:38 can be translated as "... for to him (God) all are living." God sees the future as if it is now here. Paul spoke of "God, who quickeneth (makes alive) the dead, and calleth those things which are not as though they were" (Rom. 4:17). He also wrote, *" For none of us liveth to himself, and no man dieth to himself. For whether we live, we live unto the Lord; and whether we die, we die unto the Lord: whether we live therefore, or die, we are the Lord's. For to this end Christ both died, and rose, and revived, that he might be Lord both of the dead and living."* (Rom. 14:7-9). The Lord knows which of the dead belong to Him, and these are the ones He will raise at Christ's second coming (1 Thess. 4:13-18; John 5:28, 29). The living believer in Christ need not be afraid of death because, even after death, Christ remains his Lord, who has a comprehensive record of his fidelity and plans to raise him on resurrection day.

What Does The Apostle Paul Say About Death?

What did Paul mean when he said, *'Our inner nature is being refreshed day by day'*? *"For which cause we faint not; but though our outward man perish, yet the inward man is renewed day by day".* (2 Cor. 4:16). Believers in the immortality of the soul contend that the "inward man" is the immortal soul contained within the body. This language, they claim, clearly establishes a separation between soul and body.

Undoubtedly, the Bible distinguishes between soul (or spirit) and body. According to Matthew 10:28, "soul" denotes "life" or "life principle," hence it is clearly distinct from the body. The term "soul" in Scripture does not necessarily mean what it does in Genesis 2:7, when "a living soul" includes both body and life principle (breath).

In the New Testament, the term "spirit" (Greek pneuma) refers to a person's mind or feelings. For example, in 1 Corinthians 2:11: *"For what man knoweth the things of a man, save the spirit of man which is in him? even so the things of God knoweth no man, but the Spirit of God."* Even so, no one knows the things of God except the Holy Spirit. The "spirit" in this context refers to a person's knowing component, the faculty of comprehension, or their mind.

However, in Scripture, the "spirit" or "soul" is never a distinct, immortal part of the person that resides within the body and lives on after death. Minds and emotions (spirits) cease to function after death (Eccl. 9:5, 6, 10), and the "soul" or "life" is lost when the body dies (Matt. 16:25, 26). God saves the righteous for eternal life, but the wicked for eternal death (Romans 6:23). However, as previous studies have revealed, no human has a continuous, aware life after the death of the body.

Similarly, Paul assured the Corinthians that he was "absent in body," but "present in spirit" (1 Cor. 5:3). Of course, he was not a split personality, with his body in Ephesus and his true self in Corinth. He eloquently described what it means now to say we are with someone in spirit. His thoughts, concerns, and prayers were principally directed towards the Corinthians, despite the fact that his entire existence remained in Ephesus.

Second Corinthians 4:16 plainly states that a person's inner spiritual life is refreshed day by day as he or she relies on Christ for strength to confront life's problems. Jesus stated, *"It is the spirit that quickeneth; the flesh profiteth nothing: the words that I speak unto you, they are spirit, and they are life."* (John 6:63). Every day, the Holy Spirit instills His word in our hearts (John 16:13), renewing our spiritual lives and giving us the grace to live for Christ. Ephesians 3:16-17 describes the same spiritual renewal: *"That he would grant you, according to the riches of his glory, to be strengthened with might by his Spirit in the inner man; That Christ may dwell in your hearts by faith; that ye, being rooted and grounded in love,"* . Christ lives His life through the one who receives His Spirit daily (Galatians 2:20). 2 Corinthians 4:16 does not say that the soul is immortal. It states that we must renew our inner spiritual life by turning to Christ every day.

CHAPTER 3. HEAVEN AND HELL

Is There Hell? If So, What's It Like?

Although many of us like discussing and fantasising about what Heaven will be like, who we will meet there, and what we will be able to accomplish, there is always that nagging worry that surfaces from time to time. Most people have a negative attitude regarding Hell. It's unsettling, to say the least. It frequently conjures up images of suffocating hot air, fire pits, molten lava, and the smell of sulphur. We can almost feel the heat, imagining the anguish of anyone unfortunate enough to find themselves 'down there'.

Many Christian traditions teach that if a person chooses the wrong path in life, rejecting God and what He stands for, they will die in Hell and be completely incinerated. Some of us have been horrified by this idea since childhood, seeing it as a motivator for self-control in order to avoid the doom of going 'down there'. Others have turned against God because they believe that the wicked will be burned and tormented forever. They don't comprehend how He could profess to be loving while condemning anyone who doesn't follow Him to eternal misery. They do not grasp that the wicked should be punished for their harmful actions. If you have entire confidence in Christ, there is nothing to fear: *"And whosoever was not found written in the book of life was cast into the lake of fire"* (Revelation 20:15).

According to the Apostle John's writings, Christ will reward true and faithful followers: *"Marvel not at this: for the hour is coming, in which all that are in the graves shall hear his voice, and shall come forth; they that have done good, unto the resurrection of life; and they that have done evil, unto the resurrection of damnation".* (John 5:28-29). Jesus Christ warns those around Him that when He returns, both believers and unbelievers will be in their graves. Those who have accepted Jesus as their Saviour will be revived during the first resurrection (1 Thessalonians 4:16). Those who decided to oppose Him, on the other hand, will be raised in the second resurrection (Revelation 20:12-15), which occurs after the millennium.

So, the Bible verifies that those who are unfaithful to God and refuse to follow His ways will eventually wind up in this "lake of fire." However, the Bible also teaches us something more, which many of us may not have heard before. According to Scripture, Hell was never intended for humanity in the first place. During one of his teachings in Matthew 25, Jesus told the account of God returning to earth surrounded by all of His angels. He summoned everyone who had ever lived and began dividing them in the same way that a shepherd divides sheep and goats. He sent the sheep to the right and the goats to the left. After everyone had been separated, God turned to the sheep and invited them to accept their inheritance and join Him in Heaven. Then He turned to the goats and said, *"Then shall he say to them on the left hand, Depart from me, cursed, into everlasting fire, prepared for the devil and his angels"* (Matthew 25:41).

Let me reiterate: the fire was ready for the devil and his angels. The lake of fire was never intended for humans. The all-consuming flames are meant to destroy Satan and all who follow him, the corrupted angels who sided with Satan in the struggle against God. People can only get there if they want to, if they put Satan first and refuse to obey God's rules. This is good news because it means we can choose whether or not to accept God's providence. It is ultimately our decision whether to follow God's ways and spend eternity with Him or to follow Satan's vile, selfish, and corrupt tactics.

Now that we've established that Hell is reserved for Satan and those who choose to follow him, we need to know if people who die in rebellion against God go directly to Hell or if their fates, like the resurrection of the righteous, are postponed until Jesus returns again. Will the wicked indeed be burned in Hell for eternity, subject to constant misery and suffering?

Jesus addresses similar issues in another of His parables, The Farmer and the Wheat Field. A man sowed wheat in his field, taking care of it and hoped for a bountiful harvest. However, one evening, an opponent who loathed the man crept into his field and sowed weeds everywhere before vanishing into the darkness. The wheat sprouted and expanded alongside the weeds, filling the field with both. *"So the householder's slaves came and asked him, Sir, did you not sow good seed in your field? Where did the tares come from?"* He remarked to them, *"An enemy has done this."* The servants answered to him, *"Will you then let us go and gather them?"* But Jesus responded, *"No; lest you gather up the tares and root up the wheat with them."* Let them grow together until the harvest, and then I will say to the reapers, *"Gather the tares first, and bind them in bundles to burn them, but gather the wheat into my barn"* (Matthew 13:27-30).

The context and other parables Jesus told suggest that this story was meant to provide insight into what would happen at the second coming. Up to this point, the field, or earth, has been filled by both wheat and weeds, those who follow and those who reject God. However, when Christ returns, all of this will be over. By then, the wheat will have grown sufficiently to form its own roots.

The wheat and weeds will be separated and set aside, just like in the sheep and goats story. The wheat, those who are faithful to God, will be gathered into His house, while the weeds, those who rebelled and attempted to lead others astray, will be cast into the fire. This metaphor of weeds provides the best insight into what will happen to those who reject God's will. Have you ever seen dried grass tossed onto a bonfire? It burns up swiftly, curling and withering until nothing left. It does not burn indefinitely. It fades quickly, leaving just ash. The smoke from the fire may remain long after the grass has burned, but this is not punishment. This demonstrates that the punishment has been carried out, and the wicked are no more. According to Psalm 37:20, God will remember and reward those who follow Him: *"But the wicked shall perish, and the enemies of the Lord shall be as the fat of lambs: they shall consume; into smoke shall they consume away."*

Jesus explains categorically what will happen when He returns, as well as the nature of Heaven and Hell. In fact, according to Jesus' story, Hell is more of an experience than a place, just as throwing weeds into the fire was an event. When Christ returns, He will restore order on earth. Evil and all that resulted from it will be permanently destroyed. There will be no more death or misery, and everything that has contaminated humanity will be eliminated.That includes Satan and his followers. They will suffer the destiny of the weeds in the parable, being burnt to ash until nothing remains.This is the only way. If even a trace of Satan's power is allowed to remain, it will eventually spread, and the cycle of sin and evil will begin again. God is extremely aware of this. That is why He devised the plan to eradicate evil once and for all.This is what the Bible refers to as the 'second death' (Revelation 20:6, 20:14, 21:8), which is reserved for Satan and his adherents and from which there will be no resurrection. Those who perish in the second death are indeed gone forever. Does this final cure to sin seem a little extreme? After all, isn't God the embodiment of compassion and mercy? Surely He would not allow those He made to be completely annihilated simply because they chose the wrong side of the fight.

But here's the thing: God gave those people second chances, third, fifth, and even tenth chances throughout their lives, and He has never stopped attempting to contact them. If someone chooses to side with Satan and participate in the second death, they have completely rejected God and everything He stands for. The wicked would rather experience a fleeting moment of misery and be gone forever than spend eternity with God. God demonstrates His mercy once more by taking their lives at the end of time. He loves them, and while they will never embrace His love, He will not leave them to suffer indefinitely. The end they choose will be quick, putting an end to the misery and suffering that sin has caused them. Satan will no longer be able to afflict them, and they will enjoy rest, which is all God can still provide.

Those who believe in the immortality of the soul interpret Peter's passage (1 Peter 3:18-20) in which Jesus "preached unto the spirits in prison" to mean that after Christ died, He went down to hell and preached to the bad souls who had been killed in the flood. Why would Christ do that? To give them another chance. Then they must have been in purgatory and not permanently lost! Unfortunately for this viewpoint, the Bible never indicates that those who die are granted a second chance. Consider what else Peter has to say about those who died in the flood (2 Peter 2:4–9).

When the wicked were destroyed by the flood, they were put to sleep and reserved "unto the day of judgement to be punished". The verse does not refer to Christ descending to a region of immortal lost spirits after His death; there is no such site mentioned in Scripture. For 120 years, the Holy Spirit employed Noah as a preacher of righteousness (2 Peter 2:5). The 'spirits' to whom Noah and Jesus taught were actual humans who were spiritually imprisoned because they had rejected the only true God (see Isa. 42:7; 61:1; Luke 4:18-21). The Scriptures refer to living beings on this world as "spirits" several times (Heb. 12:23, Num. 16:22, 27:16). The Bible never refers to a "spirit" (pneuma) as the disembodied, eternal spirit of a human being.

Pneuma means "wind," "breath," or "spirit." It was frequently used in the meaning of "person," or to allude to a personality trait that was inextricably linked to the individual. (1 Cor. 16:18; Gal. 6:18; 2 Tim. 4:22; compare Phil. 4:23). Just as the Holy Spirit pleaded with people before the flood, so does He plead with us today to be reconciled with Christ (1 Peter 3:18).

"Everlasting Destruction Of The Wicked"

In the New Testament, the destruction of the wicked is referred to as 'everlasting' or 'eternal.' As a result, some Bible interpreters believe that the immortal souls of the wicked will burn in hellfire for eternity. In Matthew 3:12, Jesus describes the destruction of the wicked: *"Whose fan is in his hand, and he will thoroughly purge his floor, and gather his wheat into the garner; but he will burn up the chaff with unquenchable fire." "Then shall he say also unto them on the left hand, Depart from me, ye* cursed, into everlasting fire, prepared for the devil and his angels:" (Matt. 25:41). "And these (the lost) go away into eternal punishment" , (Matt. 25: 46).

Paul described the type of destruction that will befall unbelievers: *"Who shall be punished with everlasting destruction from the presence of the Lord, and from the glory of his power; When he shall come to be glorified in his saints, and to be admired in all them that believe (because our testimony among you was believed) in that day"* (2 Thess. 1:9-10).

Do Jesus and Paul's comments imply that the wicked shall burn eternally? The answer is "no." The fire is insatiable because, like the fire that destroyed old Jerusalem, nothing can extinguish it until it has completed its task of consuming the lost. Jeremiah delivered God's prophecy to His rebellious people: *"But if ye will not hearken unto me to hallow the sabbath day, and not to bear a burden, even entering in at the gates of Jerusalem on the sabbath day; then will I kindle a fire in the gates thereof, and it shall devour the palaces of Jerusalem, and it shall not be quenched."* (Jer. 17:27). Jerusalem was destroyed, as Jeremiah predicted, and the fire was extinguished. *"And they burnt the house of God, and brake down the wall of Jerusalem, and burnt all the palaces thereof with fire. . . . To fulfil the word of the Lord by the mouth of Jeremiah. . ."* (2 Chronicles 36:19-21).

"And turning the cities of Sodom and Gomorrha into ashes condemned them with an overthrow, making them an ensample unto those that after should live ungodly," (2 Peter 2:6). However, the wicked people in those cities are no longer burning.

"For, behold, the day comes, that shall burn as an oven; and all the proud, yea, and all that do wickedly, shall be stubble." ..And ye shall trample down the wicked; for they shall be ashes under the soles of your feet in the day that I shall do this, saith the Lord of hosts" (Mal. 4:1-3). Where would the ashes come from if the wicked continued to suffer in the flames for eternity?

In the New Testament, Jesus and Paul used the Greek adjective "aionios" to describe the punishment of the wicked. However, this adjective and its corresponding noun "aion" (eternity) often refer to a limited duration, such as the current "world" or "age" that is coming to an end (Matt. 13:39; Eph. 1:21; 2 Tim. 4:10; 1 Cor. 2:2).

According to Kittel's Theological Dictionary of the New Testament, "the meaning of..." ..[Aion] combines with that of a lengthy yet restricted period of time. In particular. ..[aion] in this sense refers to the world's time or duration, i.e., time as defined by creation and conclusion. At this juncture, we are confronted with the astounding reality that the same word appears in the Bible. ..[aion] refers to two things that are fundamentally opposed to one another: God's eternity and the lifetime of the world. This two-fold sense. ..[aion] shares with the Hebrews. ...['olam] refers to the concept of eternity, which is associated with the longevity of the world."

In the New Testament, the terms "everlasting" and "eternal" may refer to a limited time period. Paul wrote to Philemon about the slave Onesimus: *"For perhaps he therefore departed for a season, that thou shouldest receive him forever;"* (Philemon 15). The term "forever" translates the Greek adjective aionios. It does not imply that Philemon would enjoy Onesimus' services for eternity, but rather that Onesimus would serve Philemon until his death.

People who are transported to heaven when Jesus returns are promised immortality (1 Corinthians 15:51-54), which means they will live eternally because immortal beings cannot die (John 3:16, 36; Matt. 25:46). What is the nature of the wicked on whom the fire is ruled at the end of the millennium? They are still mortal people, as Paul taught, *"For the wages of sin is death; but the gift of God is eternal life through Jesus Christ our Lord."* The term "eternal" in "eternal fire" refers to the limited duration of terrible agony that ends when the wicked die, which is diametrically opposed to eternal life. Because the lost are mortal, they can and will perish in the fires of the final great day.

"Forever" does not typically mean indefinitely throughout eternity. The English equivalent of "aion" or "aionios" (Greek) or "'olam" (Hebrew) denotes a finite period of time. Jonah described his time in the belly of the whale: *"I went down to the bottoms of the mountains; the earth with her bars was about me for ever: yet hast thou brought up my life from corruption, O Lord my God."* Jonah 2:6. Jonah spent three days and three nights inside the belly of a whale. Jonah 1:17. Gehazi and his children were to be lepers "forever" (2 Kings 5:27). They were lepers until death. The Israelites were instructed to observe the Passover "forever" Exodus 12:24). However, the Passover lost significance when Jesus died on the cross (1 Cor. 5:7).

These facts enable us to explain the following claims in the Book of Revelation concerning the sufferings of the wicked at the conclusion of the millennium: *"And the smoke of their torment goes up forever and ever:* [eis aionas aionon] *and they have no rest day nor night, who worship the beast and his image, and whosoever receiveth the mark of his name."* Revelation 14, verse 11. *"And the devil that deceived them was cast into the lake of fire and brimstone, where the beast and the false prophet are, and shall be tormented day and night for ever and ever"* . [Eis aionas, tonne aionon] (Revelation, 20:10). In each case, the Greek word means "for as long as the subject's nature allows." Because the wicked are immoral creatures, they suffer endlessly, which implies that their agony lasts till the end of their existence. They have no respite or relief from anguish until they are reduced to ash.

According to Jude 13 and 2 Peter 2:17, people who are 'lost will' suffer the darkest darkness "forever." What better method to convey the blackness of eternal extinction? The Psalmist stated that no one will be able to find the wicked once they have been destroyed because they will have been completely devoured. *"For yet a little while, and the wicked sha not be: "yea, thou shalt diligently consider his place, and it sha not be"* (Ps. 37:10). *"But the wicked shall perish, and the enemies of the Lord shall be as the fat of lambs: they sha consume; into smoke shall they consume away"* (verse 20).

The Hebrew word "carcasses" refers to "dead bodies" o "corpses," not "eternal souls," which are consumed by worm and fire in the new earth (Isa. 66:24). Therefore, Isaiah does no describe the redeemed as seeing disembodied immortal soul suffering in hellfire. What exactly is meant by the phrase "for their worm shall not die"? Some claim that the undying worm depicts the immortal soul. This would be an odd manner for the inspired prophet to describe the soul. In the text's Hebrew poetry, the "worm" is compared to the "fire." They are the destructive forces, not the destroyed objects. As a result, the passage's interpretation is that, as seen by the righteous, the wicked's dead bodies are still being devoured. The Hebrew verbs' simple imperfect tense suggests the following translation: "... their worm had not died yet, nor had their fire been quenched." The wicked's bodies have not yet been burned when the saved see them.

Why does Isaiah picture the saved watching the burning of the wicked's lifeless bodies? It must be realised that Isaiah's description of the new earth (Isa. 65:17 - 66:24) would have been completely fulfilled if Israel had not failed in their mission from God. Because Israel rejected Christ and the Christian Church received its spiritual blessings and evangelistic programme, Isaiah's prophesy must be interpreted in light of subsequent revelation of the new world state. Whereas Isaiah's new world for Israel included things like old age and death (Isa. 65:20). The last new world predicted by 'John the Revelator' has no suffering, death, or devastation of any kind (Revelation 21:1-5). And, unlike Isaiah's new earth, where the righteous will witness the dead bodies of the wicked, John's new earth had ultimately destroyed the wicked (Rev. 20:14, 15). The long life followed by old age and death, as well as the burning of the wicked in Isaiah's prophecy, can today be seen as metaphors for the righteous' eternal life in a world without death and no wicked people. Before the last new earth is established, the wicked will be reduced to ashes (Mal. 4:1), since their mortal souls will expire. "The soul that sinneth, it shall die," says Ezekiel 18:4.

What About Purgatory?

Purgatory, a form of in-between realm adjacent to Hell where those who have died might be prayed for, purified, and eventually welcomed into Heaven, is one of the countless conceptions we have regarding life after death. Despite its popularity, the Bible makes no reference of purgatory.

According to the Bible, the dead are completely asleep, unable to think, feel, or act. This would prohibit people from reflecting on their choices after death. When Jesus returns at the second coming, each person's decision will already be made. There will be no opportunity for people to reconsider their options and make decisions they did not make in life. Purgatory is based on the concept that one can earn their way into Heaven, despite the fact that Scripture continuously reminds us that we can only enter there by God's grace.

The concept of purgatory contradicts what the Bible says about God and the plan of salvation. Purgatory implies that we can earn our way into heaven by thinking hard enough, praying hard enough, and having others pray for us. This simply does not reflect any of the other principles given in Scripture; God is the only way into heaven, and faith in Christ is the only way to get there.

It is impossible for us to try to earn our place in Heaven. God has already provided us with a place there for free, and all we have to do is embrace His sacrifice, love Him, and live as He has asked us. That doesn't seem too difficult to accomplish, and it is much easier than waiting in Purgatory for a few hundred years, attempting to earn our acceptance or serving our time, which is equivalent to a restricted prison sentence. Christ's sacrifice pays the cost of Heaven far better than we could.

CHAPTER 4. THE RESURRECTION

The Resurrection

Earlier in the course, we discovered that the Bible, from Genesis to Revelation, consistently defines death as a state of sleep. If we are meant to fall slumber in death, it is logical that we shall one day rise in a resurrection. According to one important scripture, both the virtuous and the evil will rise again. Daniel 12:2 reads that those who sleep in the dust of the ground will awaken, some to eternal life, others to disgrace and scorn. This implies that both the just and the wicked will be revived. The Bible really says that this will happen at two different times, meaning a first and second.

During His time on earth, Jesus revealed that He had power over death, that He knew the sorrow and sadness of those who had lost loved ones, and that He would not let death end the tale. And, just as God healed and raised Lazarus, He has a plan to restore individuals who have died while believing in Him. This plan is stated in 1 Corinthians. *"But now is Christ risen from the dead, and become the firstfruits of them that slept. For since by man came death, by man came also the resurrection of* the dead. *For as in Adam all die, even so in Christ shall all be made alive. But every man in his own order: Christ the firstfruits; afterward they that are Christ's at his coming. Then cometh the end, when he shall have delivered up the kingdom to God, even the Father; when he shall have put down all rule and all authority and power. For he must reign, till he hath put all enemies under his feet. The last enemy that shall be destroyed is death.*" (1 Corinthians 15:20–26).

First, we will consider the first resurrection, which occurs when Jesus returns. If we dive deeper, we'll have to assess two important Bible scriptures. In 1 Corinthians 15:21-23, the apostle Paul outlines a series of events: *"For since death came from man, so did the resurrection of the dead."For just as all died in Adam, all will be brought alive in Christ. But each man in his own order: Christ first, then those who are Christ's at his coming."* Christ was the first fruits of the resurrection 2000 years ago, and because he was the first, the complete harvest has still to be reaped, which Paul refers to as Christ's second coming.

Christ is referred to as the "first fruits," which refers to the first product that a fruit tree produces, a foreshadowing of the vast harvest to come. Christ's resurrection foreshadowed what will happen when He returns in victory, conquering all evil, wickedness, and, finally, death itself. And with this final victory, all who died trusting in him will be resurrected, just as Jesus was. Scripture continues: "Behold, I shew you a mystery; We shall not all sleep, but we shall all be changed, n a moment, in the twinkling of an eye, at the last trump: for the trumpet shall sound, and the dead shall be raised incorruptible, and we shall be changed. For this corruptible must put on incorruption, and this mortal must put on immortality. So when this corruptible shall have put on incorruption, and this mortal shall have put on immortality, then shall be brought to pass the saying that is written, Death is swallowed up in victory. O death, where is thy sting? O grave, where is thy victory"? (1 Corinthians 15:51-55).

In 1 Thessalonians 4:16-18, Christ's plan is spelt out simply and clearly: *"For the Lord himself shall descend from heaven with a shout, with the voice of the archangel, and with the trump of God: and the dead in Christ shall rise first: "Then we which are alive and remain shall be caught up together with them in the clouds, to meet the Lord in the air: and so shall we ever be with the Lord. Wherefore comfort one another with these words."* Also in 1 Thessalonians 4:16-17, it is stated that the Lord will descend from heaven with a cry, archangel's voice, and God's trump, and that the dead in Christ will rise first. Then we who are alive and remain will be snatched up with them in the clouds to meet the Lord in the air, and so we shall always be with the Lord. We are told that the righteous will be raised from the dead at Christ's second coming, where they will meet the Lord, and we will go and live and reign with Christ alone. We will next go to heaven, where the Bible says that we will reign alongside Christ for 1000 years.

Now let us proceed to the second resurrection, which is for the wicked. Those revived in the second resurrection will face judgement. "They will die a permanent death." And death and hell were thrown into the lake of fire. "This is the second death" (Revelation 20:14). The second resurrection comes 1000 years after the first, as recorded in Revelation 20:5. The rest of the deceased, however, did not live again until the thousand years had passed. This marks the first resurrection. In other words, the virtuous live in heaven for 1000 years, and at the conclusion of that time, the Holy City, also known as the City of Jerusalem, descends from heaven, together with us in Christ, and the wicked are raised from the dead. The Bible then informs us that the wicked will surround the City in an attempt to seize it, and God will intervene and destroy them. It is said in Revelation 21:8, *"But the fearful, and unbelieving, and the abominable, and murderers, and whoremongers, and sorcerers, and idolaters, and all liars, shall have their part in the lake which burneth with fire and brimstone: which is the second death"* . Please keep in mind that this is the second death, which means that the evil will die twice, whilst the righteous will only have to go through one experience, implying that the first death is more like a sleep and hence not a true death. Remember that Jesus described death as a state of sleep, for those who truly die are cast into the lake of fire, which is a topic for another day.

People wonder what kind of body we will have in the resurrection: a physical body that is distinct from our current one, or a spiritual one. There are other points of view, and the Bible provides some clear answers on the matter. Refer to Philippians 3:21, *"Who shall change our vile body, that it may be fashioned like unto his glorious body, according to the working whereby he is able even to subdue all things unto himself"* . When Jesus was resurrected, He appeared in a new fleshly body and paid a visit to the disciples. This was recorded in Luke 24:39, *"Behold my hands and my feet, that it is I myself: handle me, and see; for a spirit hath not flesh and bones, as ye see me have"*. Notice if you will that the disciples were able touch the body of Christ and that he ate a meal with them. Next look at Revelation 22:14, *"Blessed* are they that do his commandments, that they may have right to the tree of life, and may enter in through the gates into the city". This means that if we wish to be like Christ and inherit his immortality and new body, we must also have a physical body. According to Revelation, people will once again be allowed to eat the fruit of the Tree of Life. We will need a physical body to consume fruit. We are also guaranteed that God will restore everything to its pre-fall condition. So, just as they did, we can hope to partake of the Tree of Life and other fertile trees. Life will go on as God planned.

What Is The Second Death?

Being estranged from God causes the second death, which is eternal. You may experience visions of unending sorrow and misery for lost sinners, as well as an eternal inferno where fire consumes the lost forever. So what does the Bible say? Those who die without faith in Jesus will be separated from God for eternity, rather than suffering indefinitely.If the wicked were tormented in hell endlessly, they would become immortal souls. According to John 3:15-16 and 17:3, only those who choose salvation through Jesus will get eternal life, because God is the only immortal entity. *"Which in his times he shall shew, who is the blessed and only Potentate, the King of kings, and Lord of lords; Who only hath immortality, dwelling in the light which no man can approach unto; whom no man hath seen, nor can see: to whom be honour and power everlasting. Amen"* . (1 Timothy 6:15–16).

And when the lost die a second time, they will be nothing more than ash on the ground. They are permanently destroyed, not permanently burned.The fire consumes everything; after all, a fire will naturally burn out unless it is regularly stoked. When all evil has been eliminated, the fire will be extinguished. *"Behold, they shall be as stubble; the fire shall burn them; they shall not deliver themselves from the power of the flame: there shall not be a coal to warm at, nor fire to sit before it"* . Isaiah 47:14. No one who was burned will ever come back. "For yet a little while, and the wicked shall not be: yea, thou shalt diligently consider his place, and it shall not be" . (Psalms 37:10).

When Jesus died on the cross, He experienced what the second death will be like, as well as the separation from God's presence that all the wicked will face when they die at the end of the thousand years. In the ninth hour, Jesus called out, *"Eli, Eli, lama sabachthani?"* This was a painful experience for Him. Which is why he cried out, *"My God, why have you forsaken me?"* (Matthew 27: 46).

The second resurrection enables God to judge those who perished in rejecting the gift of eternal life. Though God desires that all be saved (Ezekiel 18:31-32), He allows each individual free will and respects those who choose to reject Him. However, in order to offer a sin-free world for His people, God must annihilate all sin and sinners, including Satan and his angels.There are two reasons why the end-time resurrection is so important:

• The resurrection in the end times is inextricably linked to the resurrection of Christ. Because Jesus paid the punishment for our sin, He has made it possible for us to be raised to life someday, just as God raised Him from death.

- Without the resurrection, everyone who died in Christ is lost forever.

    Let's take a closer look at these two options.

In 1 Corinthians 15, we see a link between the 'end-times' resurrection and Christ's. According to Paul, *"But if there be no resurrection of the dead, then is Christ not risen: And if Christ be not risen, then is our preaching vain, and your faith is also vain"* , 1 Corinthians 15:13-14. One of Christians' major beliefs is that Christ rose from the dead on the third day. This belief gives us hope for the resurrection and eternal life. If the resurrection at the end of time does not take place, everyone who died believing in Jesus will perish. What exactly does "perish" mean? The Greek word for "perish," apolonto, literally means "ruined, lost, perished, and destroyed." This Greek word is also used in John 3:16, *"For God so loved the world, that he gave his only begotten Son, that whosoever believeth in him should not perish (apolonto), but have everlasting life"*. Apostle John isn't merely talking about death, which we all face at the end of our lives. It compares eternal life with eternal non-existence (death). Those who have rejected God will perish after the second resurrection, whereas God's dedicated followers will obtain what they have hoped and prayed for: eternity with God.

CHAPTER 5. SPIRITUALISM

Are Ghosts Real?

According to Deuteronomy 18:10-12, it is forbidden to use divination, enchantment, or necromancy on oneself or others.For all who do these things are an abomination to the Lord; and because of these abominations, the Lord thy God drives them out from before you." Witchcraft, sorcery, divination, and necromancy are considered abominations by God, and with good reason. The rationale is obvious: the dead are sleeping and not aware of anything. Ecclesiastes 9:5-6 states, *"For the living know that they will die; but the dead know nothing, and they have no reward; for their memory is forgotten." Also, their love, anger, and envy have vanished; they no longer have an eternal share in everything done under the sun".*

The departed have no thoughts or emotions and are incapable of engaging in any activity under the sun. If we keep this in mind, we can be certain that any attempts to interact with the dead will result in a response far more malevolent than the dead themselves. To understand what that is, read Revelation 12:9: *"And the great dragon was cast out, that old serpent, called the Devil, and Satan, which deceives the whole world: he was cast out into the earth, and his angels with him."* Read Revelation 12:4 as well: *"And his tail drew the third part of the stars of heaven, and did cast them to the earth: and the dragon stood before the woman which was ready to be delivered, for to devour her child as soon as it was born"* . In this text, "stars" represent angels, specifically Satan and his fallen angels, who revolted against God in heaven.

A third of Heaven's angels joined Satan's revolt and were cast down to Earth. As a result, whenever anyone engages with these spirits, who often resemble people we know, we must identify that we are dealing with demons or devils. These fallen angels, who have descended from Heaven with Satan, have one objective in mind: complete and utter depravity and destruction. They seek to lead us down the path of death, preventing us from experiencing the eternal life and glory that God has reserved for those who place their trust in him.

God warns us against these evil spirits because He does not want us to be misled or harmed. The dead are unconscious (Ecclesiastes 9:5-6), thus they cannot communicate or see us. That suggests that someone else is imitating those people. Peter tells us, *"Be sober, be vigilant; because your adversary the devil, as a roaring lion, walks about, seeking whom he may devour."* (1 Peter 5:8). Revelation also cautions about demonic deceptions: *"For they are the spirits of devils, working miracles, which go forth unto the kings of the earth and of the whole world, to gather them to the battle of that great day of God Almighty"* (Revelation 16:14).

Although we appear to be interacting with deceased relatives, these 'walking dead people' are deceptions; they are not our relatives. These deceptions are part of the ongoing Great Controversy between good and evil. The devil employs whatever means possible to deceive us, including this type of magic. God's warnings are just meant to protect us from what will harm us in the long run. In general, resurrection is the process of recovering life. The enormous one mentioned in Revelation occurs at the end of time, when Jesus Christ returns to earth.

When Jesus returns, the virtuous will be raised to life. The Bible refers to it as the first resurrection (Revelation 20:5), and it consists of all those who trusted in God but died before His return. They are resurrected and joined Jesus in heaven. The apostle Paul describes it as follows: *"For the Lord himself shall descend from heaven with a shout, with the voice of the archangel, and with the trump of God: and the dead in Christ shall rise first: "Then we which are alive and remain shall be caught up together with them in the clouds, to meet the Lord in the air: and so shall we ever be with the Lord"* (1 Thessalonians 4:16-17). This verse depicts our victory over the curse of sin, which has plagued all humans since Satan deceived Adam and Eve at the beginning of time. Jesus vanquished sin by dying for us on the cross, but that is the end of the story for God's people. We will receive new bodies free of illness, afflictions, and pain. These new bodies are immortal, which means they will never die again (1 Corinthians 15:53–55). Romans 6:23 states that the righteous will live forever in heaven. The Second Coming also fulfils another promise Jesus made to us: He is preparing mansions in paradise for His disciples (John 14:1-3).

We can also see in the Bible that false spirits have tremendous power. The Old Testament of the Bible, notably the book of Job, contains proof of Satan manipulating and controlling the weather, as well as sending plagues and sickness upon Job. In the Garden of Eden, the devil was able to inhabit the serpent and speak through it in order to deceive Eve. As a result, we understand that these enormously powerful beasts are beyond our knowledge, therefore we must continue with extreme caution, follow the Lord's advice, and stay a safe distance from them.

Samuel tells a story in the Old Testament on how difficult it is to interact with the dead. The plot centres on Saul and the Witch of Endor. Saul was Israel's first king, and Samuel was the High Priest during his reign. Saul began as a good monarch, hearing and accepting the Lord's message and following the path of righteousness. However, he eventually began to rebel. Saul turned away from God and distanced himself. Samuel died eventually, leaving Saul alone and estranged from God. Saul no longer had Samuel to look to for direction. As a result, in a state of desperation, Saul sought out the Witch of Endor, trying to channel Samuel's spirit through her. When we begin the narrative we will read 1 Samuel 28:8, which says, *"And Saul disguised himself, and put on other raiment, and he went, and two men with him, and they came to the woman by night: and he said, I pray thee, divine unto me by the familiar spirit, and bring me him up, whom I shall name unto thee"* . If you continue reading this novel, you will discover that the witch agrees to do this with him and summons Samuel's spirit from the ground, which appears. Saul recognises the spirit as Samuel and communicates with him. Without getting into the specifics, there are a few things to consider. The first is what we already know to be true: according to the Bible, the dead know nothing and have no ability to interact with us or influence what happens on Earth. As a result, we might argue that what we see here does not represent Samuel's spirit.

According to 1 Samuel 28:6, Saul went to the witch of Endor because he had not received a response from the Lord via dreams, Urim, or prophets. Because of Saul's continued rebellion against God, the Lord withdrew from him and cast him under the influence of evil spirits. (See 1 Samuel 16:14–16). In a conversation with the witch's summoned spirit, Saul admitted: *"... and God is departed from me, and answereth me no more, neither by prophets, nor by dreams: therefore I have called thee, that thou mayest make known unto me what I shall do"* (1 Sam. 28:15). If Saul had repented for his wickedness, God would have answered his prayers and delivered him from his adversaries. A later Bible writer explained why God took Saul's life: *"So Saul died for his transgression which he committed against the Lord, even against the word of the Lord, which he kept not, and also for asking counsel of one that had a familiar spirit, to enquire of it; "And enquired not of the Lord: therefore he slew him, and turned the kingdom unto David the son of Jesse,"* according to 1 Chronicles 10:13-14.

God had abandoned Saul and refused to answer his petitions, and God later scolded Saul for coming to the witch of Endor, thus it appears unlikely that God would use the witch to give Saul an inspired message. Since Samuel was a prophet of God during his lifetime, we can assume that the entity who appeared to the witch of Endor was an evil spirit impersonating Samuel. God was not speaking with Saul, and He never replies to prayers from mediums afflicted by evil spirits. The witch of Endor is characterised as possessing "a familiar spirit" (1 Samuel 28:7). The Hebrew term for "familiar spirit" is "ba'alath-'ob." The term "Ob" refers to a conjurer, magician, or sorcerer who professes to communicate with the dead and predict the future. God had clearly directed that such demonic spirit mediums be put to death in Israel.

Anyone who consulted spirit mediums was to be cut off from Israel. (See Lev. 19:31; 20:6, 27; Deut. 18:10, 11.) Saul had previously obeyed the divine commands in this respect by expelling the spirit mediums: "... And Saul had put away those that had familiar spirits, and the wizards, out of the land" (1 Sam. 28:3). God would certainly not speak to Saul through a witch, the very kind of person that He had commanded should not be permitted to live? Such an idea is inconceivable!

In response to the witch's incantations, "Samuel" rose, not descended (1 Samuel 28:11, 13, 14, 15). If the appearance had genuinely been Samuel's immortal soul, it would have come down from heaven rather than up from the depths of earth. The Bible writer referred to the evil spirit mimicking Samuel as Samuel solely because the tale is given as those present perceived it. Saul did not notice the spirit being. He only had the witch's word that it was Samuel (verses 13-14). Saul recognised what he "perceived" (verse 14), although not seeing the manifestation. Are we to believe a condemned witch's claim that Samuel was present? "Samuel" appeared as an elderly man who bowed with his face to the ground. Do immortal souls keep the physical appearance they had in their old age on Earth?

"Samuel" informed Saul: ". ..The next day, Saul committed suicide (1 Sam. 31:4). If he had gone to be with Samuel's immortal soul, surely he would have gone to heaven. Wicked men who are rejected by God and commit suicide do not go to heaven when they die. Saul turned away from God and consulted a medium of evil demons. Because Saul's life was in the hands of the Satan, the Satan could predict what would happen the next day.

Now lets go to Revelation 16:14, and learn what the end goal of what Satan and these fallen angels are trying to achieve, *"For they are the spirits of devils, working miracles, which go forth unto the kings of the earth and of the whole world, to gather them to the battle of that great day of God Almighty".* That Great Day alludes to the final battle of Armageddon, the final conflict between the forces of good and evil. While Christ works to seal and prepare his own people, Satan attempts to prepare another group to side with him in this great drama and revolt. We don't want to be on Satan's side, which is why it's critical that we understand miracles, spiritual events that occur to us, the appearance of loved ones, or even if an angel descends from heaven and speaks anything other than what is written in God's Word. We have to be absolutely certain we can dismiss any disinformation. We need to be able to turn away from it and trust only in God's word, especially as we know we are nearing the end, we are going to see more false miracles, false Christs, false prophets and false teachers all working wonders and signs. Let's make sure we are firmly grounded in God's word, and not deceived by these machinations, which are going to sweep around the whole world.

Chapter 6: ABSENT FROM THE BODY

Visits To Heaven

Jesus makes this clear throughout His earthly ministry. When Jesus resurrects Lazarus and the centurion's daughter, he describes them as "asleep." This does not apply in certain situations, such as when God transports a person to Heaven. For example, the Bible says Enoch and Elijah are in Heaven (Genesis 5:24, 2 Kings 2:11), and Moses appears at the transfiguration in Matthew 17:1-9. While we don't know why these chosen few are transported to paradise right away, we do know that we may trust God's plan, timing, and actions. Elijah, an Old Testament prophet, was transported to heaven in a chariot of fire while still alive (2 Kings). He appeared to Jesus many hundred years later, before he was executed (Luke 9:28–36).

Another example is Moses, who died on his route to Canaan (Deuteronomy 34), yet he did not stay in the grave for long. The New Testament suggests that he was resurrected. Jude 9 recounts a conflict between Satan and Michael, the archangel, for Moses' body. In Luke 9, Moses was also present when Elijah came to Jesus. All of this shows that Moses was not immediately taken to heaven after death, but rather raised as a foreshadowing of God's people's eventual resurrection.

Today In Paradise

Jesus' remarks to the thief on the cross are frequently cited as the reason why people believe that when they die, they immediately go to Heaven. Let's look at a specific passage in scripture that we discover in Luke 23:43, *"And Jesus said unto him, Verily I say unto thee, Today shalt thou be with me in paradise"*. A quick perusal of this verse reveals how people could believe that Jesus is teaching that both He and the thief will ascend into Heaven on that exact day. However, as we looked into the subject of death, we discovered that the Bible never teaches that when we die, we go straight to Heaven.

This article has successfully shown that death is an unconscious state of slumber. So, how do we reconcile what we've already learned with what Jesus seems to be saying in this situation? The answer is that the New Testament was initially written in Koine Greek, the most frequently spoken and understood language in the Eastern Mediterranean region at the time, and the disciples used it to write many of their writings. What we need to know about Koine Greek is that it lacks punctuation marks. Punctuation was added later by Bible translators who worked from ancient Greek to modern languages. What happens when Luke 23:43 is translated as *"verily I say unto thee today, thou shalt be with me in paradise"*? A comma has been added after the word 'today', and it conveys a completely different meaning. Instead of informing the thief that both He and the thief will be in Heaven on that specific Friday, Jesus says, *"As I am here with you today, I promise that I will remember you when I come into my kingdom, and you will be with me there, one day"*.

How do we know that the comma goes after the word 'today'? There are two ways to determine this. The first step is to understand what we've been learning, so let's review everything we've learned so far. The second method for verifying the punctuation in the final Bible passage is to read John 20:17, Jesus says to Mary, *"Do not touch me because I have not yet ascended to my Father: but go to my brothers and tell them that I am ascending to my Father, and your Father, and to my God, and your God."* What Jesus is telling Mary now is that he has not yet ascended into Heaven.

Remember that this conversation takes place on Resurrection Morning; hence, if Jesus died and went to Heaven with the thief on Friday, how could he possibly appear to Mary on Sunday and declare that he had not yet ascended to Heaven? He'd be lying, unless the comma was in the wrong place. When we consider that the comma should be placed after the term 'today', we can see that what Jesus genuinely said to the thief is fully compatible with what else is mentioned in scripture, as well as everything we have already studied about the dead. The dead are sleeping till the resurrection. It also conforms to what Christ told Mary, in that he had not yet ascended into Heaven. We can conclude from this narrative that what Jesus says is consistent with what is written: He promises to recall the faithful thief at the set time of His second coming and raise him up to bear with Him in Heaven for all eternity.

The Apostle Paul

Contrary to common belief, we do not instantaneously ascend to Heaven upon death. One scripture in particular causes confusion: 2 Corinthians 5:8, *"We are confident, I say, and willing rather to be absent from the body, and to be present with the Lord"*. When we read this line in isolation, it appears to infer that some part of us will split from the physical body and ascend into Heaven to dwell in the presence of God. But is this what Paul is actually teaching? In other places, Paul has repeatedly indicated that death is a state of sleep that we will remain in until the resurrection. If we examine all of Corinthians chapter five, beginning with verse one and drawing on the appropriate context, we will realise that Paul is teaching the same thing in this particular paragraph.

Beginning with verse one, read it piece by piece and understand what Paul is truly saying. According to 2 Corinthians 5:1-4, *"For we know that if our earthly house of this tabernacle were dissolved, we have a building of God, an eternal house not made with hands, eternal in the heavens"*. In verse one, Paul talks about two different houses: the earthly house and the eternal Heavenly house that God will provide. Paul is also referring to our physical or earthly body, and we will someday have a glorified, eternal body. Then, in verse two, Paul adds, *"In this earthly body we groan because it decays, breaks down, and dies."* We age, suffer from disease and illness, and groan in our bodies, longing to be clothed in the abode of Heaven.

Moving on to verse three, Paul introduces another concept: being naked between earthly and heavenly mansions. We died, thus we no longer have a physical body. Keep in mind that our deceased bodies return to the dust from which they originated, leaving us bare. Paul goes on to say that he dislikes the concept of being naked. Paul is looking forward to acquiring the Heavenly refuge, an eternal and immortal body in which he would be able to live eternally in Heaven.

Earlier in the Bible, Paul teaches us when we will acquire this Heavenly body, 1 Corinthians 15:52-54, *"In a moment, in the twinkling of an eye, at the last trump: for the trumpet shall sound, and the dead shall be raised incorruptible, and we shall be transformed. Because this corruptible must become incorruptible, and this mortal must become immortal. So, when this corruptible has become incorruption and this mortal has become immortal, the saying, "Death is swallowed up in victory,"* will be fulfilled. We are told that when Christ returns, we shall be given our Heavenly home. That is the eternal and immortal body that we will take to Heaven and keep for many years to come. This reveals that we currently have an earthly home and an earthly body that is in pain and dying, leading us to moan. We are also in the position of being nude, without a body, which Paul insists he does not want. Paul longs for the Heavenly House because it promises eternal and immortal life.

Paul stated, *"We are confident, I say, and would prefer to be away from the body and at home with the Lord."* (2 Cor. 5:8)? Those who believe in the immortal soul cite this verse (2 Cor. 5:1-10) to indicate Paul's desire to be a disembodied spirit in heaven. The context implies otherwise. He refers to three alternative states: (i) "our earthly house" (verse 1); (ii) the "naked" or "unclothed" condition (verses 3, 4); and (iii) God's building, an eternal house not constructed with hands and eternal in the heavens. The "unclothed" state is a transitional phase between the terrestrial and heavenly states. In the earthly condition, the believer has an earthly body. In the celestial realm, he will have an immortal and unchanging body. However, in the "naked," or "unclothed" condition, he will have no body at all because God has reduced it to dust and removed the vital essence. As we have seen, this life force is not a conscious, immortal entity.

Paul predicted the resurrection of the body at the second coming (Romans 8:11, 22, 23; Philippians 3:20, 21; 1 Corinthians 15:4-44). His emphasis was not on retaining a disembodied spirit after death, but on joining Christ on the resurrection morning (2 Tim. 4:8; 1 Cor. 15:51-54). Paul remarked, *"For to me, living is Christ, and dying is gain. If I continue to live in the body, I will be able to work productively. But what shall I choose? I don't know! I am split between the two: I want to leave and be with Christ, which is far better; but, it is more important for you that I remain in the body"* (Phil. 1:21-24). He does not, however, state in this verse when he will be with Christ. In terms of the dead, the interval between death and resurrection when Christ returns is quite brief. Following death, he realises he is in the presence of Christ. As a result, Paul's readiness to lay down his life was not driven by a wish to live on as a disembodied soul in heaven after death. It was in light of his desire to be raised and join Christ on the resurrection day.

Being without a body and shedding it meant entering God's presence in a spiritual condition. However, Paul makes it plain that he does not want to be naked, but rather clothed with the Heavenly House. With that in mind, let's move on to the more challenging verses. Next, read 2 Corinthians 5:6, *"Therefore we are always confident, knowing that, whilst we are at home in the body, we are absent from the Lord:"* . What is Paul referring to in this verse? While we are in this physical body, we are not permitted to be in the presence of God. We should interpret this to suggest that the physical body is decaying due to sin and sickness. This stops us from coming into the presence of the holy, glorious, and righteous God. While we remain in the physical body, we are not in the Lord's physical presence.

Moving on to the text at hand, let's interpret what we've learned. 2 5:8 says, *"We are confident, I say, and willing rather to be absent from the body, and to be present with the Lord"* . Paul emphasises his longing to be free of this earthly body, recognising that we cannot carry it to paradise to live with the Lord. Paul makes it clear that he does not wish to be naked or without a body. Paul understands that there is no remembrance of God after death. In the grave, no one thanks God. Paul believes that there is no cognition or experience in death. Please examine the following scriptures: Ecclesiastes 9:5, Psalms 146:4, Psalms 6:5, and Psalm 115:17.

For Christian believers, death is a condition of unconsciousness followed by eternity with Christ, and resurrection is an eternity of restfulness. Hopefully, you now understand that Paul is not teaching that there is a spiritual part of us that separates from the body at death and enters the presence of God, which contradicts the message Paul was delivering. What greater blessings could the Lord bestow on us?

How Do We Reserve A Place For Ourselves In Heaven?

The Bible acknowledges the agony of losing loved ones, but understanding death and the resurrection that follows gives us hope. Even if we die, our faith in Jesus gives us hope for life after death. Jesus assures us in John 11:25–26, *"Jesus said unto her, I am the resurrection, and the life: he that believeth in me, though he were dead, yet shall he live: And whosoever liveth and believeth in me shall never die. Believest thou this?*

When we devote ourselves to Him, He desires nothing more than to preserve and ensure our eternal existence. However, the actions we make today will determine whether we receive eternal life. God loves us and respects our freedom to choose. He helps us understand our options by explaining death and resurrection in Scripture, allowing us to choose our fate. He does this to get us ready for the resurrection of life. By making that decision for Him, we get security for the future. Jesus vowed to come for us. And He will keep the promise.

- Believe in the name of Jesus Christ.

- Recognise that you are a sinner in need of salvation.

- Recognise that the consequence for sin is death.

- Ask God for pardon and repent of your sins.

- Accept Jesus as your personal Saviour and follow Him.

Once you've accepted Jesus as your personal Saviour, you must respond to what God has done for you by living a life like Christ's. We want to be like Jesus not just for salvation, but because we adore Him. Jesus is our model! We can live Christlike lives by following the Bible's guiding principles. Here are some of the principles: *"Meekness and temperance: against such there is no law."* (Galatians 5:23)". *"Finally, brethren, whatsoever things are true, whatsoever things are honest, whatsoever things are just, whatsoever things are pure, whatsoever things are lovely, whatsoever things are of good report; if there be any virtue, and if there be any praise, think on these things"* , Philippians 4:8 says. *"A new commandment I give unto you, That ye love one another; as I have loved you, that ye also love one another"* , (John 13, 34). Christians are called to be a light in their communities. Wherever you go, folks should notice a reflection of Christ in you. Let us follow Jesus' example of peace and love!

After the final death of the unfaithful, God will create a new world free of sin and death. God's people will live without pain or suffering. God will govern from His throne, and we will all live in perfect harmony in an endless paradise. The Bible depicts a lovely city filled with precious stones and gold as pure as glass, with the Tree of Life in its core. *"And I saw a new heaven and a new earth, for the old heaven and earth had passed away, and there was no longer a sea. And I John saw the holy city, new Jerusalem, coming down from God out of heaven, prepared as a bride adorned for her husband"* (Revelation 21:1-4).

If you want to be a part of the first resurrection, you must connect with God. Accept Jesus as your salvation today. *"For God loved the world so much that he gave his only begotten Son, that whoever believes in him should not perish but have everlasting life"* (John 3:6). You can live a faith-filled life and become one of God's loyal people at the end of time by praying and studying the Bible! *"For the Lord loves judgement and does not desert his saints; they are kept forever, but the seed of the wicked will be destroyed. "The righteous will inherit the land and live there forever"* (Psalm 37:28–29). Reading God's Word will help you learn more about Him. As you study the Bible and pray, you will form a bond with Him. You can accept Jesus as your Saviour and follow Him in a few easy steps. It'll be the best decision you ever make! *"That if thou shalt confess with thy mouth the Lord Jesus, and shalt believe in thine heart that God hath raised him from the dead, thou shalt be saved"* , Romans 10:9, emphasis added.

The best part of all is that when we accept Jesus as our Saviour, we are no longer terrified of death. While we may have natural emotional reactions to death and dying, the idea of Jesus Christ's Second Coming can provide us with calm. As 1 Thessalonians 4:14 explains, *"For if we believe that Jesus died and rose again, God will bring those who sleep in Jesus with him."* And those of us who have lost loved ones during our time on this earth may find solace in the fact that, according to the book of Revelation, *"And God shall wipe away all tears from their eyes; and there shall be no more death, neither sorrow, nor crying, neither shall there be any more pain: for the former things are passed away"* (Revelation 21:4).

We've lived among sin, sorrow, and death, encountering both good and evil as our human nature chose via Adam and Eve in the Garden of Eden. However, God never intended for this to be the conclusion of humanity's story. When He returns to take us home, He will make everything right, and those who have died will awaken to the most beautiful sight. God is gracious in ending the wicked's misery. Jonah must have felt as if he had spent an eternity in the belly of the whale. And the afflictions of the departed will appear to continue forever. However, the Lord is too loving and gracious to let them suffer continuously, forever.

Are you willing, like Stephen the disciple, to entrust your life to the eternal Life Giver? The Lord implores you to reject fables in favour of the truth of His Word and find your assurance of salvation in Christ. The concept of soul immortality exposes spiritism's deceptions, as well as the errors of purgatory and eternal damnation. We can rejoice because God's Word sets us free from these deceptions and fallacies. And we can rejoice because Christ died to deliver us from sin and devastation. *"For God so loved the world that he gave his only born Son, so that whomever believes in him will not perish but have everlasting life"*. (John 3:16).

Praise the Lord that each one of us can have a share in the planet made new where sin, misery, and death are no more!. If we die before Jesus returns, we will be restored and given eternal life (1 Corinthians 15:51–54). If we live until His return, we will be immortal and have the opportunity to spend eternity in a cosmos free of the curse of evil, AMEN.

CHAPTER 7: THE TRANSFIGURATION OF CHRIST

Ascending To The Light

Luke places the transfiguration eight days after a lengthy ministry and teaching cycle that includes the twelve disciples being sent out to preach, the five thousand being fed, Peter's confession, and a lesson about the cost of following Jesus. In the gospels, we regularly see Jesus spending time in prayer with His disciples after such intense moments of action. About a week after warning His disciples that He would suffer, be crucified, and raised (Luke 9:22), Jesus led Peter, James, and John to a mountain for prayer.

Luke begins the narrative with a detail that Matthew and Mark do not mention: Jesus accompanied Peter, John, and James up the mountain to pray. Jesus fixed His gaze and concentration on Jerusalem, anticipating the path of pain that lay ahead of Him. Jesus is demonstrating that prayer is the only method to gain faith and assurance. The act of praying instantly poured out divine glory on Jesus: *"His face was altered, and His robe became white and glistening"* (Luke 9:29). This praying period takes place during Jesus' transfiguration in Luke 9, Matthew 17, and Mark 9. It said: *"As He prayed, the appearance of His face was altered, His robe became white and glistening."* (v.29). The term "glistening" literally means "emitting light," which suggests a bright flashing light. What a beautiful scene! This astonishing incident didn't end there; the three disciples saw two men chatting with Jesus, Moses, and Elijah!

The transfigured Jesus was talking to Moses and Elijah about *"Who appeared in glory, and spake of his death, which he would accomplish at Jerusalem."* (Luke 9:31). Although the Greek word used here, exodus, is not typically associated with death, "decease" can also relate to the great "exodus" that Jesus was about to do in Jerusalem, the mighty redemptive exodus that would bring about deliverance from sin.

While praying, His personal appearance changed into a glorified form, and His clothing became bright white. According to Matthew 17:1-13, Mark 9:2-10, and Luke 9:28-36, Jesus' transfiguration marked a turning point in his mission. The Transfiguration provides another evidence that Jesus was God's holy Son. It's no accident that this happened immediately after Jesus announced Himself as the Christ, the one who left heaven's glory to come to Earth. Three of His disciples were supposed to obtain a glimpse of His brilliance. In the eyes of Peter, James, and John, Jesus temporarily abandoned His human appearance to reveal His divinity. The Father's voice then pierced the sky, announcing His satisfaction with His son, Jesus. The experience was so powerful for those who observed it that Peter verifies its authenticity in his epistle (2 Peter 1:16-18).

The scripture, on the other hand, may perplex individuals who understand that when people die, they sleep in preparation for a physical resurrection when Christ returns. To make sense of this, we must first understand two fundamental notions. The first is that, while God's people will be resurrected in their entirety at the end of time, individual resurrections are recounted in the Bible. For example, Christ's resurrection did not fit under the generic category. Neither were the saints who rose from the dead after Christ's resurrection (Matthew 27:52–53). During their ministries, the prophets Elijah and Elisha both performed resurrections. Individual resurrections throughout history do not invalidate the general resurrection when Christ arrives.

The second foundation to understand is that some people have gone to Heaven without dying and hence do not require a resurrection. After a long day of teaching and ministering to the public, Christ and His disciples separate from the clamouring crowds. Then he says something odd: *"And he said unto them, Verily I say unto you, That there be some of them that stand here, which shall not taste of death, till they have seen the kingdom of God come with power."* (Mark 9:1) Jesus is hinting towards the cataclysmic events that are about to unfold.

Six days after Jesus' mysterious pronouncement, they arrive at the foot of a "high mountain." There, He handpicks His trusted "trinity" of apostles, Peter, James, and John, and leaves the rest in the valley to undertake the difficult trip up the steep hill. They finally arrive at the summit, tired, as the sun sets. Jesus immediately kneels and begins to pray, and the disciples rush to join Him; however, exhausted, they quickly fall asleep.

Then something spectacular happens! According to Luke and Mark, "As Jesus prayed, He was transformed in front of them." His face altered, and His garment turned a brilliant white and glistened excessively. (for the full account see Luke 9:29-31 and Mark 9:2-9). The three-way discussion concluded with a word of approval from heaven: *"And there came a voice out of the cloud, saying, This is my beloved Son: hear him."* (Luke 9:35). The Transfiguration anoints Jesus with glory, confirms His

Sonship once more, and announces that Redemption would require the Son's life. As a result, the heavenly command to the disciples is: listen to Him. There is no discipleship without complete obedience to Jesus.

At the time of the Transfiguration, Jesus' earthly ministry was coming to an end. He had acknowledged that He was the Messiah and predicted His death and resurrection, and now He was about to reveal His divine glory to a select few. The Transfiguration also symbolised Jesus' power over death and his

A Divine Discussion

But how did Peter and (probably) the other two disciples know that Moses and Elijah were speaking with Jesus? Some have commented on their appearance, but there could be more at work here to help us understand how they were identified. First and foremost, all three gospels situate Jesus' revelation as "the Christ, the Son of God" eight days before His transfiguration. Second, and more likely, the identity of the two individuals speaking with Jesus was revealed as they conversed with the Lord. The gospel of Luke is the only witness to what the two men discussed with Jesus: Jesus' departure. The Greek word "exodos" is the fundamental term for "decease" (KJV) or "departure" (ESV). This implies that Moses (who led the people of Israel in an exodus from Egypt) and Elijah (who died in a fiery chariot) spoke with Jesus about His future "exodus" via His death on the cross and resurrection from the grave. This is most likely how Peter realised it was Moses and Elijah speaking with Jesus.

How fitting that these two people should return to earth to encourage Jesus to continue His sacrifice. Both Moses and Elijah understood the agony of persecution and rejection by their own people. Keep in mind that Moses and Elijah had been in heaven for hundreds of years, not because of their good deeds, but because they were receiving an advance payment for Jesus' impending sacrifice. In other words, if Jesus did not carry out the purpose of dying for humanity, Moses and Elijah had no right to remain in heaven. They were clearly enormously motivated by Jesus' exhortation to press forward. Finally, their objective was to be witnesses for Christ and to accompany Jesus on His upcoming trial and sacrifice.

The Reason For The Revelation

Undoubtedly, the goal of Christ's transfiguration into at least some of His heavenly splendour was to give the "inner circle" of His disciples a fuller knowledge of who He was. Christ underwent a tremendous alteration in appearance so that the disciples may view Him in His glory. The disciples, who had only known Christ in His human form, had a better sense of His divinity, but they still didn't fully grasp it. That provided them with the reassurance they needed following the devastating news of His approaching death.

The apparition of Moses and Elijah represented the Law and Prophets. But God's command from heaven, "Listen to Him!" made it clear that the Law and Prophets had to make way for Jesus. The One who is the new and living way replaces the old; He fulfils the Law as well as many of the Old Testament's prophesies. Furthermore, they saw a foreshadowing of His eventual elevation and enthronement as King of kings and Lord of lords. He is no longer the humble son of Joseph and Mary, but the majestic Creator of the universe, unveiled in all of His glory.

The Glorious Mount experience is the ultimate endorsement. Since Abraham's day, the Israelites have been waiting for the Messiah. As a symbol of unrivalled support, Jesus is now glorified, flanked on the right and left by two of ancient Israel's finest prophets. Moses and Elijah surround Jesus, providing a vivid picture of how God's Word recognises and supports Jesus as the Messiah. This endorsement refers to God's Word, the law, and the prophets confirming Jesus as the "coming one" (Matthew 11:3). No one could have supplied more confirmation for Jesus' work than these two biblical giants. The transfiguration is the direct fulfilment of prophecy by Malachi 3:1 & 4:4, *"Behold, I will send you Elijah the prophet before the great and dreadful day of the Lord." "Remember the law of Moses, my servant, which I commanded at Horeb for all Israel, with the commandments and judgements."* One of the reasons God's Word is so amazing is its accuracy. Moses and Elijah appeared in the New Testament before Jesus' sacrifice to encourage and support Him.

The loving Father grants them this brief glimpse of His Son's glory because He knows the disciples will shortly experience their Master's humiliation. Their teacher was willing to be stripped naked, beaten, and tortured, seeming defenceless and mortal. As a tree in nature reserves sap during the warm, beautiful spring to support itself throughout the cold, dark winter, Jesus sees that His disciples' confidence needs a tremendous boost on the mountain to see them through the approaching dark day on Calvary. This experience also instilled faith in the disciples, who had previously confused the goal of the Messiah's mission with typical Jewish tales of earthly splendour. Jesus knew it would be heartbreaking for them to have their dreams of worldly greatness smashed by Roman nails, so the Father gave them this vision to warn them that Christ's kingdom was heavenly, not earthly.

In biblical terms, the Transfiguration has been seen to have various crucial implications for Jesus' active ministry. For starters, it established Jesus' divine identity as God's Son by providing visual confirmation of his descent from heaven to earth. Second, it confirmed Jesus' victory over death and the future resurrection. Third, it provided more evidence to both the disciples and the Jewish officials that Jesus was the Messiah and King.

Furthermore, the Transfiguration demonstrates Jesus' great power. In Matthew 17:1-5, Moses and Elijah appear before Jesus and the three apostles, Peter, James, and John. A radiant cloud swept over them at this point, accompanied by the words, *"This is my beloved Son, in whom I am well pleased;"* (Matthew 17:5). This event was intended to reveal that Jesus had come from God to fulfil his role on earth as the Messiah foretold by multiple Old Testament prophets and anticipated in the New Testament.

The Transfiguration also symbolised hope for Jesus' resurrection. In Matthew 17:9, when questioned why Moses and Elijah were present at the Transfiguration, Jesus says, *"And as they came down from the mountain, Jesus charged them, saying, Tell the vision to no man, until the Son of man be risen again from the dead."* This word promised his disciples that he would overcome death through his resurrection.

The famous work 'The Desire of Ages' (pp. 419-421) by Ellen White helps us understand Jesus' main purpose for this angelic visitation. According to Jesus, "He pleads that they may witness a manifestation of His divinity that will comfort them in the hour of His supreme agony, with the knowledge that He is ... the Son of God and that His shameful death is a part of the plan of redemption.".

Mountaintop Experience

The actual location of the Transfiguration is uncertain, according to the Bible. However, it is likely that it occurred on Mount Tabor, a high mountain near Capernaum in Galilee, Israel. Jesus may have chosen this location because it had special meaning for him, as he frequently went out into the highlands to pray. The Transfiguration is considered to have occurred about six days after Jesus revealed himself to be God's Son at Caesarea Philippi (Matthew 16:13-16). Many of the Bible's high points are about mountaintop experiences. The Lord frequently staged significant events on mountaintops, which serve as natural monuments. When God's people saw these towering heights, they remembered major events from their sacred history.

Consider how, after forty years in the wilderness, God revealed His covenant to Moses on a mountaintop. Mount Sinai was ablaze with God's fire, with smoke and thunder roaring from its summit. After 40 days in the desert, God used fire, wind, and an earthquake to communicate with Elijah on Mount Sinai (1 Kings 19:11-12). After 40 days in the wilderness, Jesus confronted the demon on a high mountain (Matthew 4:8-10). God also makes commitments on the mountains. God established His covenant with Noah on the heights of Ararat. He made a covenant with Abraham on Mount Moriah. The entire Jewish tribe confirmed its Promise Land commitment from Mount Gerizim (Joshua 8:33). Of course, Elijah was on Mount Carmel when fire and rain fell, representing God's revitalising Spirit on the church. Moses viewed the Promised Land from Mount Nebo, whereas John sees the holy city from a high mountain in Revelation 21:10. Most importantly, God confirmed his love covenant of salvation at Mount Calvary.

Moses, like Jesus, stood on a mountain with his hands extended, supported to the right and left by Aaron and Hur (Exodus 17:12). In reality, as Jesus died on Calvary, two thieves surrounded him from the right and left, representing two sorts of sinners, exactly as Moses and Elijah did on the Mount of Transfiguration. Before any of us can reach the Glorious Mount, we must first climb Mount Calvary. God desires to confirm a covenant with you and fill you with His Spirit, but only if we humble ourselves on the mountain where Jesus died.

Moses And Elijah At The Transfiguration

You may be wondering, why these two people? Simply said, the two essential people who arrived were living examples of God's Word. The appearance of Moses and Elijah with Jesus is hugely significant. The name Moses was associated with the Old Testament law that God had given to Israel. Jesus came and fulfilled the law's requirements while also doing things the law could not, such as offering an answer to the problem of sin. The Torah identified the problem, whereas Jesus gave the solution.

In Jewish tradition, Moses and Elijah represent two aspects of life: Moses represents the law, and Elijah represents the prophets. In Matthew 5:17, Jesus says, *"Think not that I am come to destroy the law or the prophets: I am not come to destroy, but to [fulfil]."* Moses is the greatest lawgiver because the law was delivered through Moses, but grace and truth came through Jesus Christ (John 1:17), and Elijah is the greatest Old Testament prophet. Elijah never died. He sees believers entering God's kingdom through the translation or rapture of the church. Elijah was a prominent figure in the Old Testament. He was a well-known prophet, and his appearance alongside Moses on the Mount of Transfiguration demonstrated that Jesus fulfilled both the prophets and the law. Elijah symbolised prophecy, according to Malachi 4:4-6. The Transfiguration showed Jesus' divinity as the fulfilment of both law and prophecy.

When we recognise the significance of this event in light of what Moses and Elijah represent, we have a greater understanding of death. If everyone went to heaven to live in

Christ's presence immediately after death, there would be no need for a physical resurrection; similarly, translation to heaven would have no distinct meaning because everyone would go to paradise right away. Moses and Elijah show how death creates unconsciousness, while the sleeping saints await the return of Jesus Christ.

While the transfiguration does not reveal any direct knowledge regarding the status of the dead, it does have theological significance. When Peter reported his experience in 2 Peter 1:16-18, he said he saw Christ arrive at that time. In other words, he saw the event as the return of Jesus Christ. Moses and Elijah represent the two groups of God's people who will be present at that miraculous event: Moses represents the "dead in Christ" who will be raised to new life, and Elijah represents "those who are alive and remain" who will be translated to heaven and eternal life without ever experiencing death (1 Thessalonians 4:16). The understanding that the transfiguration indicates Christ's second coming helps us appreciate Christ's promise that *"some standing here ... shall not taste death till they see the kingdom of God,"* stated a few days before the transfiguration (Luke 9:27).

According to 2 Kings 2:11 and Jude 9, Elijah was taken to paradise without having died first. According to verse 11, he was caught up in a celestial whirlwind and taken to heaven in front of his successor, Elisha. Elijah's arrival with Christ during the transfiguration is perfectly appropriate; he had spent a great deal of time with Jesus in heaven before His human birth in Bethlehem.

Moses, on the other hand, died in the wilderness before guiding the Israelites to the Promised Land. The tale of his death, contained in Deuteronomy 34:5, 6, reveals something remarkable. According to the Bible, God Himself buried Moses, and no one in Israel knew where he was interred. This is the first scriptural clue that Moses will experience something unusual after death.

In contrast, the New Testament contains additional material. In Jude 9, we discover that the archangel Michael fought Satan for Moses' body. In other words, Satan claimed Moses as his own, demanding death along with everyone else. However, Michael had a different point of view. As the archangel, He has the power to revive God's people. (See 1 Thessalonians 4:16; the archangel's voice raises the dead in Christ when He returns.) Moses was not supposed to die. He was raised from the dead and has been living in heaven ever since. Truly, he has lived beyond death. As a result, Moses and Elijah's presence during the transfiguration does not provide an answer to the question "What is death?" because neither were dead! Elijah never felt death, and Moses had a new life after his resurrection, just as Christ's followers will when He returns.

Many respectable Christians believe that in the end times, Moses and Elijah will literally return to earth to preach, only to be slain and left in the streets for three and a half days. It's a misnomer because the 'two witnesses' are only symbols for Moses and Elijah. These two men of God are in heaven with glorified bodies, and the Bible makes no mention of God intending to slay two others. Moses and Elijah will not return to Earth in this fashion. Throughout the Bible, the Word of God is frequently depicted in a dual image. The 10 commandments were written on two stone tablets. The word of God is also shown as a sword with two edges. Two lamps and two olive trees symbolise the Bible's two sacred divisions. But Jesus is the final testament to God's Word: *"Then said I, Lo, I come (in the volume of the book it is written of me,) to do thy will, O God."* (Hebrews 10:7). The volume of the Book, the Bible, all point to Jesus, who combines two natures: human and divine. Jesus is the Word Made Flesh (John 1:14).

Since we're talking about the end times, let's look at one major issue that is causing a lot of uncertainty. Revelation 11:3 cites two witnesses. *"And I'll give power to my two witnesses, and they will prophesy one thousand two hundred and sixty days, clothed in sackcloth."* Please keep in mind that this does not mean that these two witnesses will just prophesy for 1,260 days; God's witnesses testify at all times. This, of course, refers to the Dark Ages, which spanned from AD 538 to 1798 and concealed the law and prophets, commonly known as the Scriptures.

Ellen G. White stated that these men, referring to Moses and Elijah, who had been *"chosen above every angel around the throne,"* had come to speak with Jesus about the scenes of His suffering and to comfort Him with the assurance of heaven's sympathy. *"The load of their interview was the world's hope, the salvation of every human being."* (The Desire of Ages, p. 425). So, even Jesus, who had comforted so many people, sought consolation and comfort for himself. What does this teach us about how even the most spiritually powerful people, such as our leaders, instructors, and guides, may benefit from the comfort, support, and aid of others? You know probably know somebody right now who might use some peace, comfort, and encouragement.

Two Or Three Witnesses

Revelation 11:3-12 provides a stunning prophecy from God's two witnesses. *"These are the two olive trees and the two lamp-stands standing before the God of the earth"* (Revelation eleven:4-5). We know that a lamp signifies God's Word: "Your word is a lamp to my feet, and a light to my path" (Psalm 119:105). When Zechariah sees two olive trees in a vision, he asks the angel what they represent. *"Then he answered and spake unto me, saying, This is the word of the Lord unto Zerubbabel, saying, Not by might, nor by power, but by my spirit, saith the Lord of hosts."* (Zechariah, 4-6). It also needs olive oil from the Spirit to light the lamp of God's Word.

Revelation foreshadows what would happen to those who destroy God's two witnesses, the Holy Bible. *"If anyone wants to hurt them fire proceeds out of their mouths and devours their enemies."* This happened in the lives of both Elijah and Moses. As the Egyptians pursued God's children, fire descended from heaven and consumed Aaron's sons. It also engulfed the warriors that confronted Elijah. In addition, *"These have the power to shut up heaven so no rain falls in the days of their prophecy; and they have power over water to turn them to blood."* Did Elijah pray and the rain stop? Did Moses pray, and the water became blood? So we can see why God compares the two witnesses, His Word, to the ministries of Moses and Elijah.

Then, as if Moses and Elijah's endorsement weren't enough, a cloud overshadows the mountainside, and the Almighty's voice is heard saying, *"This is My beloved Son, Hear Him."* The Bible states, *"This is the third time I am coming to you. In the mouth of two or three witnesses shall every word be established."* (2 Cor. 13:1). On the Mount, two humans who have been redeemed by Christ declare that He is the Messiah, while the third is the voice of God! What higher assurance of truth could God have given the lawgiver, the greatest prophet, and His own auditory testimony? In effect, Moses says, "This is the One." Elijah says, "This is the one." Then God Almighty says, "This is the one."

Transfiguration Fortells Crucifixion & Resurrection

The Transfiguration was a crucial foreshadowing of Jesus' suffering and resurrection. As Peter observed this time with Jesus, he acquired insight into what would happen later in his life. This gave Peter and the rest of us hope that Jesus' death would have a lasting influence on our lives. The Transfiguration of Jesus continues to inspire and motivate believers today. It is an example of what happens when we allow God to act in and through us. This pivotal biblical episode also reminds us that, no matter how tough life appears, we can keep our faith in the face of adversity by turning to Jesus for courage, healing, and wisdom.

It Represented His Coming Kingdom

Jesus' Transfiguration symbolises the entirety of His future kingdom. Jesus Himself addressed His people. *'I tell you the truth: some of you will not die until they see the Son of Man enter his kingdom"* (Matthew 16:28). First, the Transfiguration demonstrates that God communicates with those who trust him. Moses and Elijah were conversing with Jesus on the mountain, but they were also communicating directly with the Father via his Son. This was a great demonstration of how God enjoys receiving our pleas. If we invite him into our hearts, we may be confident that he will always be there to support and guide us through difficult times.

We also learn from the Transfiguration that God wants us to concentrate on him and Jesus' words. Peter agreed to build three shelters probably because he was overwhelmed. Nonetheless, God used this opportunity to remind us of Jesus' identity and what He planned to do for humanity's salvation. There is nothing to fear in him because He truly cares about us.

The Final Word

The cloud lifted, and Moses and Elijah withdrew, leaving Jesus alone with His apostles, who were horrified. Jesus instructed them not to tell anybody what they had experienced until after He had risen. Matthew 17:1-8, Mark 9:2-8, and Luke 9:28-36 all provide accounts of this event. The Glorious Mount resounds with heavenly authority. The Bible states in Mark 9:7, *"And there was a cloud that overshadowed them: and a voice came out of the cloud, saying, This is my beloved Son: hear* him." This veil completely obscures the glory of the Father, who declares, *"This is My beloved Son.Hear him."* God the Father comes to sanction His Son, who has His complete approval. This is extremely crucial for us to grasp. God the Father speaks personally to Jesus at His baptism in the low Jordan valley, identifying Him as His Son. He declares, *"This is My beloved Son, in whom I am well pleased,"* implying that the Jewish people no longer need to look for anybody else as the Messiah (Matthew 3:17). Anyone who came before Him was a fraud, and anyone who comes after is a counterfeit. Jesus is the One!

Then, near the end of Jesus' mission, God the Father recognises His divine Son on the mountain and issues a simple mandate. "Hear Him." That's a comprehensive and understandable sentence. But "hear" refers to more than just auditory noises. It essentially means "listening with undivided attention and doing." Jesus says, "He who has an ear, let him hear what the Spirit says to the church" (Revelation 2:17). God the Father is personally directing you and me to hear and obey Jesus' words. There have been several counterfeiters, fraudsters, imposters, and cult leaders striving to imitate Christ. However, God the Father says of Jesus in the Bible, "Hear Him." He is the true Word! That is an incredibly convincing thought.

Suddenly

According to Mark 9:8, "Suddenly" everything came to an end, and the light turned on and off almost as quickly as it came on. *"When they had looked round about, they saw no man any more, save Jesus only with themselves."* As the splendour fades and their eyes adjust to the darkness, Moses, Elijah, the Father, and the cloud vanish; all they see is Jesus.

The kaleidoscope of images we see in the Bible and the collage of images we see in modern life can cloud our vision, but what really matters after it all fades and we're at the base of the mountain again? God is telling us to only hear Jesus, to only see Jesus, because he was the only one left with them; everyone else might abandon you, but Jesus says, *"I will be with you till the end"* (Matthew 28:20).

Don't Mention It

We can't imagine how the three apostles felt "as they came down the mountain" (Mark 9:9). It must have been a life-changing event, and they were most likely in spiritual shock, more so than when Christ calmed the storm or walked on water. They might even have been glowing from the residual light that had dissipated from their faces, as Moses had been after speaking with God.

They have just seen a glimpse of heaven, seen Moses and Elijah, heard God's commanding voice reverberating from a mountain, and now Jesus tells them not to tell anyone about what they've seen. This may have been one of the most difficult commands they've ever received from their Lord.

Timing To Tell

Fortunately, they were not instructed to "never mention it." More specifically, Jesus asked, (Mark 9:9). Why would Jesus make this request knowing how deeply their hearts had been touched by this event? In all probability Jesus wanted them to keep this experience in reserve for when they really needed it.

Peter, James, and John were chosen to be the leaders of the early church, and when

Did God give you a summit experience? Perhaps He answered prayers and performed miracles that made you say, "Wow, praise the Lord!" But when the splendour fades, you're left in a valley with the devil overshadowing you, and the recollection of what happened on the mountain is all but gone. It's similar to when God commanded the children of Israel not to build idols, and they heard his voice, felt the ground tremble, and saw fire consume a mountain, they glibly promised the Lord that they would obey, but a few days later, they're worshipping a golden calf.

The devil is a master at producing mountaintop amnesia; if you give him even five minutes of your attention, he can make you forget a lifetime of wonders. If you accept his ideas, embrace his discouragement and doubts, all those summit memories may evaporate just when you need them the most.

Last-day Significance

The episode on the Glorious Mount is exceedingly crucial for the end times, which is why Jesus came after His resurrection to preach about it. And beginning with Moses and all the prophets, here are Moses and Elijah again! He expounded to them in all the scriptures the things concerning himself" (Luke 24:27; Luke 24:28).

In Revelation 12:17, it is written, *"And the dragon was wroth with the woman, and went to make war with the remnant of* her seed, which keep the commandments of God, and have the testimony of Jesus Christ." The woman represents the church, and the dragon, or devil, seeks to destroy her. The church in the end times has two distinguishing characteristics: they "keep the commandments of God, and they have the testimony of Jesus." What is Jesus' testimony?

Isaiah 8:16 reads, "Bind up the testimony, seal the Law among My disciples." Before his death, Moses exhorted the children of Israel to observe the law, and in Deuteronomy 5 he repeats the Ten Commandments to them, stating, "These words that I have spoken unto you today shall be in your heart." You'll link them to your hand. "They will be like frontlets between your eyes." As a result, the Holy Spirit instills the law and prophetic words in the brains and hearts of God's people. "And grieve not the holy Spirit of God, whereby ye are sealed unto the day of redemption" (Ephesians 4:16, 17).

We must immerse ourselves in the law and the prophets, in God's Word, for a special purpose in these final days. According to Mark 9:3, "And his raiment became shining, exceeding white as snow; so that no fuller on earth can white them." Mark is unable to depict the dazzling aura of light that the disciples beheld surrounding this celestial assemblage. Christ's attire was bright white, like fresh snow, and shined like the sun. Of course, the robe Jesus wore symbolised His purity. That is what He is wearing in paradise. If we follow His Word, we will be given the same clothes that has been cleaned with His blood. "And I said unto him, Sir, thou knowest. And he said to me, These are they which came out of great tribulation, and have washed their robes, and made them white in the blood of the

Lamb." (Revelation 7: 14). *"Since you have purified your souls in obeying the truth through the Spirit in sincere love"* (1 Peter 2:12).

A Type Of The Second Advent

To complete the circle, let us briefly return to where we started. One of the most important takeaways from the Mount of Transfiguration is that it shows a miniature form of Jesus' second coming. Referring back to this episode, Peter interprets it as a foreshadowing of Jesus' arrival. *"For we did not follow cunningly constructed myths when we told you about the power and coming of our Lord Jesus Christ, but were eyewitnesses to his majesty. For he gained honour and glory from God the Father when the glorious glory spoke to him, saying, "This is my beloved Son, in whom I am well pleased."* (2 Peter 1:16, 17).

Moses, who died and was resurrected (Jude 1:9), represents the kind of saints who will be alive and resurrected when Jesus returns. Despite the fact that these disciples passed away a long time ago, they were given an early glimpse of what it will be like when Christ returns. During the transfiguration, Jesus, Moses, and Elijah are dressed in white garments similar to those worn by the redeemed; clouds of glory accompany them; Jesus departed in the clouds and promised to return in the clouds; and the voice of the Father in heaven can be heard on the Glorious Mount, just as it will when Christ returns to the Father's right hand (Matthew 26:64).

Six Days To Come

The fact that this occurs six days after Jesus promises the disciples that they will see his Kingdom arrive may be significant. We were told He waited six days before taking them up the mountain, but before we continue, both Matthew and Mark recount this period as six days, while Luke says the delay was eight days. Many enemies like to point to this and say, "Contradiction!" However, this is not the case. Matthew and Mark, both Jews, recorded time in a different manner than Luke, who was Greek. Luke provides the day Jesus spoke of the occurrence, the time it took them to return home, and a rough estimate of "about eight days." As a result, these three accounts are perfectly compatible.

However, after six days, Jesus leads the disciples up. As we read in 2 Peter 3:8, *"But, beloved, be not ignorant of this one thing, that one day is with the Lord as a thousand years, and a thousand years as one day."* Following Adam's fall, God promises that Christ will come to vanquish the devil, and when Christ does, He promises to return. If we can estimate the date of creation to be around 4004 BC, we can conclude that God spoke via the patriarchs for 2,000 years, including Adam, Methuselah, Enoch, and Noah. Abraham was born in the year 2004BC. God utilised the Israelite nation, the Hebrews, to spread His gospel throughout the next 2,000 years. They waited patiently for the Messiah to emerge via their descendants. Then, around 4 BC, Jesus Christ was born, and for the last 2,000 years, God has proclaimed His good news to spiritual Israel, the church. These three 2,000-year intervals add up to 6,000 years. If we apply Peter's concept, we can conclude that we are living in the end times. The verse continues, *"For a thousand years in thy sight are but as yesterday when it is past, and as a watch in the night."*

According to the Bible, the Lord promises that the virtuous will live and reign with him for 1,000 years, a restful Sabbath. Following this time in heaven, God establishes a new heaven and earth, from which New Jerusalem will descend. We should not be surprised if we find ourselves nearing the end of the Probationary Period, assuming we are not already there, because the Bible states that the Lord is long-suffering and does not want anyone to perish.

A Biblical Theme

In Job 5:19, it is stated that *"He shall deliver thee in six troubles: yea, in seven there shall no evil touch thee."* In addition, Athaliah reigned for six years before Josiah was coroneted. When Josiah emerged from the temple, Athaliah was killed, and he was anointed; the trumpets sounded, and the Sabbath began. Jesus proclaims, "I am the sower." Similarly, the earth will be desolate for a thousand years, during which the gospel will not be sown, just as Hebrew servants were liberated after six years of service and abandoned their fields on the seventh. "The gospel is the seed." In Revelation, He appears holding a sickle, ready to harvest.

The most fascinating aspect is when Moses stayed at the foot of Mount Sinai. We all know that Jesus stayed on the mountain for 40 days and 40 nights, just like the flood. But first, Exodus 24 says, *"For six days he stayed at the base of the mountain."* After that, God summoned him to the summit to receive the commandments. This is just like what happened on the Glorious Mount. After six days, Jesus ascended the mountain, where Moses welcomed him. The Bible goes perfectly together! It's like a puzzle. It is intriguing that it says "after six days." This implies, if this is a miniature symbol of the second coming, we are getting very close to the Lord's return.

The Tranquillised Church

It is vital to recall that the Glorious Mount appeared completely unexpectedly. This should serve as a sobering reminder in our current predicament. Satan appears to appease the saints at key moments in Christian history. According to Luke 9:32, the disciples "were heavy with sleep" right before the revealing of glory. According to the Bible, when Jesus visited the Garden of Gethsemane, He chose the same three disciples to join Him in prayer. They slept again. Similarly, in the parable of the ten virgins, Jesus warns us just before his second coming that "while the bridegroom tarried, they all slumbered and slept." Matthew 25:5. The saints appear to be sleeping throughout Jesus' most important periods of ministry. For this reason, Jesus warns, *"Watch ye therefore: for ye know not when the master of the house cometh, at even, at midnight, at the cock crowing, or in the morning: Lest coming suddenly he find you sleeping."* (Mark 13:35, 36).

When they should have been kneeling with Him in the garden, contemplating the beauty they had witnessed, they fell asleep. And because Peter, James, and John were sleeping on the Mount of Transfiguration, they missed the entire extent of their experience. They had forgotten the Glorious Mount, so they were unprepared to accompany Christ to Mount Calvary. The memory of it must have haunted them for the rest of their lives: a missed opportunity because they slept rather than prayed.

In Luke 16:31, Jesus concludes His parable of the Rich Man and Lazarus: *"And he said unto him, If they do not hear Moses and the prophets, neither will they be persuaded, though one rose from the dead."* Here, Jesus places a high emphasis on God's Word, which we should not ignore. Regardless of the miracles you see, including someone rising from the dead, you should always prioritise the plain Word of God.

A More Sure Word

The disciples never forgot what happened on the mountain, as was clearly intended. In John's gospel, he wrote, *"And the Word was made flesh, and dwelt among us, (and we beheld his glory, the glory of the only begotten of the Father,) full of grace and truth."* Peter also wrote about it: *"For we did not follow cunningly concocted tales when we told you about the power and advent of our Lord Jesus Christ, but were eyewitnesses to his majesty. For he gained honour and glory from God the Father when he heard the wonderful glory say, "This is my beloved Son, in whom I am well pleased." And we heard this word from heaven while we were with him on the holy mount* (2 Peter 1:16-18). Those who witnessed the transfiguration bore witness to it for the other disciples, as well as countless millions over the centuries.

So, how can we stay awake? We can supplement the powerful weapon of prayer with the testimony of Moses and Elijah, the law, and the prophets. God's Word can prepare you for anything. In 2 Peter 1:17-18, Peter mentions the Glorious Mount again. This is the only time the three disciples have written about it. But before Peter dies, he writes passionately,

"For he received honour and glory from God the Father, when there came such a voice to him from the excellent glory, saying, This is my beloved Son, in whom I am well pleased." We heard this voice from Heaven when we were with Him on the holy mount.

Even after reflecting on that pivotal moment in his life, Peter says, *"We have also a more sure word of prophecy; whereunto ye do well to take heed"* (v. 19). Can you imagine saying that after experiencing Christ in all of His glory in the company of two of the greatest Old Testament characters, with God the Father's voice etched in your mind forever? However, Peter concedes that, as beautiful as that experience was, he had something more important and dependable. The Word of God "grows brighter and brighter until the day dawn."

Peter saw Christ glorified and caught a glimpse of Heaven. But you and I own something more valuable. We own a Bible. Christ shows us through Peter that the Bible is more trustworthy than visions. If you want to have a summit experience, reach for your Bible. Nothing is more important than Moses and Elijah's testimony, the double-edged sword, the Law and Prophets, God's commandments, and Jesus' testimony; it is the most valuable gift God has given to humanity. Jesus, the Word, became flesh.

Significance Of Transfiguration

The Transfiguration of Jesus is, without a question, central to Christian theology. This miraculous event, in which Jesus underwent a spectacular metamorphosis in front of three of his devoted disciples, demonstrated Jesus' authority over all creation and revealed his identity as the long-awaited Messiah sent by God to restore humanity. At this time, we see what awaits us after our earthly death: eternal life, spiritual strength, and heavenly happiness. Finally, the Transfiguration permits us to contemplate Christ's magnificence and apply its spiritual truths to our daily life.

The Lord has sent us a special warning message from the Mount of Transfiguration. There will be some really difficult days ahead, and we must spend time on the mountain gathering light from God's Word to help us navigate the dark valleys. The message from the mountain proclaims that Jesus is the One and that we, too, can wear the robes that He, Elijah, and Moses were arrayed in on that occasion. He encourages us to listen to Jesus' testimony, as well as the laws and prophets, which all point to Christ's fulfilment. It depicts Jesus' impending second coming and acts as a warning against spiritual slumber. The mountaintop experience reminds us that even after the splendour fades, Jesus is with us and the only way to heaven.

The Transfiguration is notable because it depicts the majesty of Jesus' body. Those who were with Him witnessed Jesus' entire glory. The apparition of Moses and Elijah confirmed that Jesus was the one referred to in the law and prophets. God the Father's affirming testimony established Jesus' identity. Seven persons arrived on the mountain that day: three from heaven (Moses, Elijah, and God the Father), and three from earth (Peter, James, and John). Then there was Jesus, the bridge and ladder that joined heaven and earth.

CHAPTER 8. OUT OF BODY EXPERIENCES

Near Death Experiences And Christianity

What occurs after we die generates a sense of wonder. As our society's Christian fabric unravels, many people are looking for solutions beyond the grave in areas where the Bible has already testified. Numerous interviews, studies, and papers about near-death experiences have come together. This phenomena has become so widespread that it has a scientific name: Near Death Experiences (NDEs). Though NDEs are still contentious, many dramatists have used them to support the immortality of the soul and the belief that, after death, the soul moves on to another state of conscious existence. The European Academy of Neurology examined participants from 35 countries who claimed encounters similar to a near death experience. They discovered that one out of every ten persons have had a near-death experience.

In recent decades, a profusion of books, videos, and documentaries have been created pertaining to stories concerning persons who "died" in the sense that they suffered cardiac arrest and stopped breathing, only to be resuscitated and restored to consciousness. Many of these folks have described remarkable experiences of conscious existence after they had supposedly "died" in numerous instances. Some claimed floating in the air and being able to see their own bodies beneath them from above. Others experienced floating out of their bodies and encountering a magnificent entity filled with light and warmth who spoke truths about kindness and love. Others described meeting and communicating with deceased relatives.

While we know there is a lot of interest in near-death experiences, how do we approach them as Bible-believing Christians? What are these phenomena? Does the Bible mention them? How can we distinguish between fact and fiction? In essence, how should Christians understand near-death experiences?

According to those who examine the phenomenon in the medical world, NDEs are often positive experiences. Unfortunately, not all near-death experiences are positive. Nancy Evans Bush, President Emerita of the International Association for Near-Death Studies, and Bruce Greyson, MD, co-authored a 2016 National Institutes of Health article titled "Distressing Near-Death Experiences: The Basics." Bush and Greyson explain, "The vast majority of near-death experiences (NDEs) reported publicly over the last four decades have been described as pleasant, even glorious. Almost undetected in the euphoria surrounding them has been the sobering fact that not all NDEs are so up-lifting. Some are very unsettling. Few people are forthcoming about such an event; they hide; they disappear when asked for information; if they are an inpatient, they are likely to withdraw; they are under a lot of stress." It's not surprising that distressing NDEs aren't as well publicised in a culture that appears to be more focused on positive messages. Because traumatic near-death experiences are more difficult to document, it is risky to speculate on how many NDEs are positive or negative based on accounts.

What Is A Near-Death Experience (NDE)?

Scientific Medicine defines an NDE as "a common pattern of events that many people experience when they are under intense threat, seriously ill, or on the verge of death." NDEs can consist of the following reported experiences:

- A strong brightness
- Previews of Future Events
- Quickly working, sharp minds
- Comfortable sensations without pain
- Remembering significant past occurrences
- Sensation of being pulled into darkness or a tunnel
- Feelings of tranquilly, well-being, or unconditional love
- Encounters with deceased relatives, friends, or religious figures
- Sensations of leaving the body, with the ability to observe one's own physical body

However, NDEs are yet another example of one of "the two great errors". As long as someone believes that the soul continues to live in some form after death, they are vulnerable to most occult or spiritualistic deceptions, which can easily promote the concept that you don't need Jesus, either explicitly or implicitly. In fact, most people who have had NDEs have reported that the spiritual beings they met, or even their deceased relatives, comforted them with words of love, peace, and goodness but said nothing about salvation in Christ, sin, or future judgement, the most fundamental biblical beliefs. One would imagine that, while apparently experiencing the Christian afterlife, they would have gained a grasp of the most fundamental Christian beliefs as well. However, what they've experienced frequently sounds like New Age ideology, which could explain why many of these people are less attracted towards Christianity than they were before they "died".

Lawrence Den Besten, a surgery professor, recounted his experience during a speech in Pasadena, California. He went on to recount his experiences during the brief period when he was near death. He saw himself lying in his coffin, as well as everyone who passed by it. Then, *"I suddenly realised that I was being held by my feet." My head was beating violently, and I coughed. For 47 years, I've dwelt on these memories. Now I understand. ..I was having a normal dying experience."*

In 2015, the film 90 Minutes in Heaven was released. It was presented as the true story of Don Piper, a victim of a severe car accident who was proclaimed dead at the scene but eventually recovered in the hospital. He then told others around him that he had a near-death experience in which he saw God in a blinding bright light in the heart of heavenly Jerusalem. Piper saw and heard the voices of many other Christians who were on their way to heaven. After he recovered from his injuries, he began to share his stories and reassure people that paradise exists.

We are not dealing with a frivolous fringe issue, but rather with a serious worldwide problem. Raymond A. Moody, Jr.'s book, Life After Life: 'The Investigation of a Phenomenon — Survival of Bodily Death' (Atlanta, GA: Mockingbird, 1975), presented the results of a five-year study of over one hundred people who experienced 'clinical death' and were revived, as one of the most popular modern arguments to "prove" the theory of the natural immortality of the soul. Prior to their rebirth, several individuals reported to have seen a kind and warm entity of light. This has been described as "exciting evidence of the survival of the human spirit beyond death" (back cover).Many similar books have been released over the years, all pushing the same notion.

Read the resurrection accounts in 1 Kings 17:22-24, 2 Kings 4:34-37, Mark 5:41-43, Luke 7:14-17, and John 11:40-44. How many of them discuss any form of conscious existence while the resurrected ones were dead, and why is this answer significant?

Modern literature reports near-death experiences of people who are clinically dead but not truly dead, unlike Lazarus, who was dead for four days and his corpse was decaying (John 11:39). Neither Lazarus nor any of the biblical individuals who were resurrected mentioned any afterlife experience, whether in Paradise, Purgatory, or Hell. This is, certainly, an argument from silence, but it is entirely consistent with biblical teachings on the unconscious state of the deceased!

But what about the "near-death" experiences that are so widely reported today? If we accept the biblical teaching of the unconsciousness of the dead (Job 3:11-13, Psalm 115:17, Psalm 146:4, Eccles. 9:10), we have two main possibilities: it is a natural psycho-chemical hallucination under extreme conditions or it is a supernatural satanic deceptive experience (2 Corinthians 11:14). Satanic deceit could be the explanation especially because several of these folks claim to have spoken to their deceased relatives! However, it could be a combinatio of both causes. With this deception so common and persuasive to many, it is critical that we remain steadfast in our commitment to the teachings of God's Word, regardless of any experiences we or others may have that contradict what the Bible says.

Facts And Fiction About Near Death Experiences

There are evil people that have a strong interest in spreading this story. After all, there is a lot of money in so-called "heavenly tourism." In 2010, Kevin and Alex Malarkey wrote The Boy Who Came Back from Heaven. The duo described the NDE of a six-year-old (Alex) who was crippled in a horrible accident and was expected to die. Alex claims to have visited paradise, seen angels, heard otherworldly music, and met Jesus while comatose in a hospital. The book sold over one million copies. It turns out that it didn't happen.

Five years after publication, the young author recanted his story, despite the fact that his father continued to profit from it. In an open letter to booksellers, Alex admitted that he made it up to gain attention. The story was a lie. 'Lifeway Christian Stores', one of the largest booksellers of the fable, eventually removed the remaining copies from the shelf, but not before hundreds of thousands of people believed a story told by a youngster named Malarkey.

Obviously, we cannot believe every near-death experience. Some people who describe NDEs may be driven by attention, such as Alex. Others can have a financial motivation. The 2014 film 'Heaven is for Real' was about a young boy who became unconscious during emergency surgery, allegedly visited heaven, and met deceased loved ones with Jesus. The movie grossed more than $100 million! This is not to say that the film was not based on a true occurrence, but we must acknowledge that there are financial incentives to promote a captivating near-death experience, even if there are other seemingly beneficial results or reasons to convey the narrative.

Christians should prioritise truth over any confirming experience in an NDE (John 8:32). After all, we don't need anecdotal evidence to confirm what we already know from Scripture. When we come across a potentially believable testimony of someone who may have experienced a near-death experience, we must compare it to more solid sources. Here are three scriptural questions that will help determine whether a near-death experience is authentic:

• Is the person typically reliable (Luke 16:10)?

• Was there a long-term, beneficial change in the person's life as a result of the NDE, which relatives and friends can attest to (Deuteronomy 19:15-21)?

• Does the NDE match what Scripture says about the experiences described (2 Peter 1:19)?

Answering yes to all of these questions suggests a near-death experience. However, answering these questions does not imply that a near-death experience happened. If any of the events or descriptions contradict what we know to be plainly taught in Scripture, we must dismiss the narratives or attribute them to other malevolent reasons. Finally, we should not rely on an imperfect person's subjective experience with eternal matters.

Near Death Experiences In The Bible

When we get to the Bible, we discover only a few references to near-death experiences. Scripture contains at least 10 accounts of persons being raised from the dead. Some of these resurrections include Elijah raising the son of the Zarephath widow from the dead (1 Kings 17:17-22), the dead man who was raised when his body touched Elisha's bones (2 Kings 13:20, 21), Jesus rising from the dead (Matthew 28:5-8; Mark 16:6; Luke 24:5, 6), and Dorcas being raised from the dead (Acts 9:36-41). The remarkable thing about these people who returned is their lack of knowledge about the other side. This is not to say that they didn't have any unique experiences. However, with the exception of Jesus' post-resurrection testimony, the Bible contains no words from persons who have had an NDE.

The closest thing we uncover to a near-death experience in Scripture is Stephen's martyrdom in the book of Acts. In Luke's account, we read about a stressful situation preceding death which often accompanies NDEs in the scientific literature: *"But he, being full of the Holy Ghost, looked up stedfastly into heaven, and saw the glory of God, and Jesus standing on the right hand of God, And said, Behold, I see the heavens opened, and the Son of man standing on the right hand of God. Then they cried out with a loud voice, and stopped their ears, and ran upon him with one accord, And cast him out of the city, and stoned him: and the witnesses laid down their clothes at a young man's feet, whose name was Saul. And they stoned Stephen, calling upon God, and saying, Lord Jesus, receive my spirit. And he kneeled down, and cried with a loud voice, Lord, lay not this sin to their charge. And when he had said this, he fell asleep".* (Acts 7:55–60)

In this story, Stephen's eyes are open to events in heaven shortly before he is killed. This supernatural revelation revealed a celestial panorama in which the Trinity was both active and visible. Stephen, guided by the Holy Spirit, saw both Jesus and God the Father in heaven. Because this occurrence is documented in Scripture, we know that a near-death experience can provide glimpses of a true heaven. In other words, authentic near-death experiences are feasible and could be utilised by God because they are consistent with Scripture.

Materialistic Explanations For Near-Death Experiences

Despite the widespread interest and literature on near-death experiences, atheistic materialists have attempted to dismiss the phenomenon. Materialists believe that matter is all that exists, hence immaterial souls do not exist, nor does a spiritual realm. Materialists propose numerous reasons for near-death experiences, including physical anomalies.

Dr. Peter Fenwick is a consultant neuropsychiatrist at the Maudsley Hospital in the United Kingdom, where he also serves as the president of the International Association for Near Death Studies. Fenwick created a database of more than 300 NDE accounts. The Christian Medical Fellowship examined the findings and discussed several typical materialist explanations for near-death experiences, as well as why they do not always work.

Unlike NDEs, hallucinations are known for their subjective nature. Despite some parallels to hallucinations, NDEs are more diverse and involve cultural components not always found in chaotic hallucinations.

Drugs: Drugs are frequently delivered as part of a resuscitation effort, which might disrupt brain activity and cause an NDE. However, just 14% of the patients in Dr. Fenwick's database received medications during their experience.

Endorphin-related: The body's own pain-killing endorphins may generate bliss, resulting in an NDE. For example, there is an increase in endorphins following grand mal seizures, but the effect is seldom good, and coherent visions are rarely observed.

Cerebral hypoxia: Some have proposed that low oxygen levels may trigger random firing of neurons in the visual system. This experience may result in a centre dot of light spreading out to the periphery of vision, giving the appearance of travelling down a tunnel of light. However, those who suffer cerebral hypoxia in other contexts (such as fighter pilots) do not have NDEs.

Though some near-death experiences can be explained away by materialistic explanations, it is impossible to reconcile hundreds of otherworldly experiences in an atheistic and materialistic universe. On the other hand, NDEs are easier to interpret from a Christian perspective in a universe created by

God, filled by immaterial souls, and formed alongside other spiritual creatures and realms such as heaven and hell.

Biblical Truth Transcends NDEs

As with everything else, the Bible is the most reliable source of information about this life and the life to come. Near-death experiences are inherently subjective events that occur to an individual. God knows why they occur. If they are from him, they may be intended for a specific individual. Perhaps God will use such an occurrence to lead others to him. Though some may be accurate, we cannot be confident about any specific NDE. Subjective experience must never trump the explicit teaching of God's Word, which is our only reliable foundation.

The Apostle Peter stated, *"We have also a more sure word of prophecy; whereunto ye do well to take heed, as unto a light that shineth in a dark place."..*" (2 Peter 1:19). Peter reminds us that the "prophetic word" will validate our experiences. This includes near-death experiences. This applies to our own NDEs "visions," and so on, as well as the experiences of others.

In terms of what we can expect when we die, the Bible says that everyone is appointed to die and will be judged (Hebrews 9:27). The only way to gain God's favour is via Jesus who said, "Jesus saith unto him, I am the way, the truth, and the life: no man cometh unto the Father, but by me." (John 14:6) *"For God so loved the world, that he gave his only begotten Son, that whosoever believeth in him should not perish, but have everlasting life."* . (John 3:16). These things are certain.

Conversely, near-death experiences are less certain. After all, we live in a spiritual realm. Fallen angels can mislead people, including Christians. Paul cautions the Corinthian believers of Satan's machinations in 2 Corinthians 11:14, writing, "And no marvel; for Satan himself is transformed into an angel of light."

A near-death experience appears to bring individuals closer to the spiritual realm. So, in a near-death experience, people can be misled by hostile spirits who appear kind but are actually out to deceive them. This arena might be Satan's playground, as he is the "prince of the power of the air" (Ephesians 2:2). Because NDEs may be influenced by demonic forces, our interpretation of them must be grounded in Scripture.

Near-Death Experiences Indicate Certain Death

Finally, near-death experiences allude to an unavoidable reality: death. Since Adam and Eve sinned in the Garden of Eden (Genesis 3:1-7), everyone who has lived before us has died. Death is one of humanity's unifying forces (Romans 5:12). NDEs pique people's interest in a world where everyone dies.

Near-death experiences suggest a realm beyond our own. It can be difficult to determine whether a specific near-death experience is a genuine God-given event. However, one thing is true for everyone: we shall all die. And there is only one way to avoid a just and eternal judgement: repent and believe the gospel of Jesus Christ.

CHAPTER 9. BEREAVEMENT

What Does The Bible Say About Grief?

Few things diminish one's happiness and health like losing someone. Grief, whether it be the death of a loved one, an unexpected illness, or the loss of a profession, may plunge us into new levels of despair. In such cases, questions often arise. Why did this have to happen? Is there any chance for me now? Is there anything to cling to when it seems like everyone has abandoned me? Where was God when I was hurting?

Grief is a lonely feeling that may cause us to question our own motivations for living. However, Scripture shows that there is light in the darkness. Although this struggle can be terrible at times, the Bible shows the hope offered to individuals who are suffering with a heavy heart. With the Bible as our guide, we'll look more closely at:

- What it truly means to grieve.

- Finding optimism during the grief process.

- More hope is supplied via Christ.

- People grieved in the Bible, and God reacted.

- While grieving, we can take comfort in Bible promises.

- The remedy to grief is our hope for the future through Jesus.

The Bible's teachings on grief can give us with consolation and peace in the power of Almighty God. It shows an awareness of Christ's compassionate love and compassion for all of His injured children. So let's see what we find.

Grief And Mourning

The entrance of sin into the world causes loss, broken relationships, and a bleeding heart. Furthermore, the Bible indicates that death came into the world as a result of sin (Romans 5:12). Was sin and death God's original goal for His creation? The answer is a massive no. It wasn't. In reality, a Bible scripture declares that Jesus' goal was to offer us abundant life.*"The thief cometh not, but for to steal, and to kill, and to destroy: I am come that they might have life, and that they might have it more abundantly."* (John ten:10).The "thief," often known as Satan, is responsible for all of the world's pain and poisoned pleasures. He created death and the pangs of loss that have deprived many people of the delight of life.

When God created us, He intended for us to live abundantly. Why? Because love is at the heart of His character, He constantly acts on it (1 John 4:8). However, God gave us free will so that we could enjoy abundant lives. This indicates that, rather than being robotic, He granted us the ability to choose. And this freedom of choice wasn't without consequences. The dangers of rebellion and disobedience. The first rebel was Satan, and his fall introduced sin and sorrow into the world, which is why Christ came. His mission was to assist those who were suffering as a result of sin and death. And to restore His creation to the life He intended for them from the moment He created us.

What Is Grief?

It is a state of deep depression and mental suffering induced by the consequences of sin. And why do we regret our loss? We grieve and react to loss because it is not something we were meant to experience. We know in our hearts that losing people to death is wrong. It isn't supposed to be like this. Things like your son's death or a family member's positive cancer test results were never God's plan. According to 1 John 4:8, "God is love," and humanity was made in God's image (Genesis 1:27).The idea is that God's original plan was for us to give and receive love. In light of this, it is very logical that we lament a loss. It's the feeling we experience when we lose something we cherish and love, sometimes unjustly. This experience leaves you feeling empty. Furthermore, it breaks God's heart.

This is abundantly portrayed in the Gospel of John chapter 11, where Lazarus dies. According to Scripture, "Jesus wept" upon arriving at Lazarus' funeral. According to Ellen White, a well-known Adventist author, the Creator of the universe weeps. Despite being the Son of God, Jesus took on human nature and was affected by human suffering. His sympathetic, pitying heart is constantly aroused to sympathy by pain; He weeps with those who cry and rejoices with those who rejoice (Desire of Ages, p. 533).

According to Psalm 34:18, God is near to the brokenhearted and saves those who are crushed in spirit. What a striking image of hope and a revelation of God's goodness!

There Is Hope In The Midst Of The Grieving Process

The process of mourning and grieving the death of a loved one falls into five major categories. Some people may go through all five, while others just go through a handful. They include:

- **Denial:** is a shock reaction that occurs when someone suffers or perceives loss. During this time, a common response may be, "This isn't happening!" or "This can't be happening!"

- **Anger:** At this stage, your emotions take over, and you may feel a rush of despair. Typically, the "why" questions arise during this phase. Unlawful sentiments are frequently directed towards everyone involved in the situation, some of whom may not be at fault.

- **Bargaining:** This is the period of remorse. For example, in the event of death, one may reason, "If only we had gotten the tests earlier, she would still be here." In the event of a job loss, "If only I had worked more overtime, they would've seen my value." You may argue that if something had happened sooner, everything would have been fine. This typically leads to feelings of dissatisfaction with yourself or others, which sets the stage for the next step.

Depression: At this point, many people isolate themselves. They may need time to process everything that has happened. Emotions catch up with them, and they may feel heavy and disoriented. This stage could last just a few days or years.

- **Acceptance:** At this moment, you have accepted what has happened in your life. This does not mean that the suffering will go away or that you will be completely free of "tough days." However, you have recognised the truth of the situation.

The majority of people who have lost someone in their lives experience these five phases of bereavement. And God provides a healthy way to handle these seasons in the Bible. When you believe you've hit your limit, there are promises of hope and strength to keep you going.

During these times of sorrow, scripture reminds us of a beautiful truth: we are not alone. Jesus understands what we are going through (Hebrews 2:14-16). And He is not an impersonal God who watches us from afar.

God's heart is overwhelmed with pain as He witnesses the struggles of people who have lost someone. Our grief inspires his heart to compassion (Hebrews 4:14,15). And we can be confident that He is with His grieving children (Psalms 34:18). So, in the midst of loss, we should not wonder where God is because He promises to always be with us. Your previous current situation may seem overwhelming, but knowing that God is with you is reassuring. He is not indifferent to your sorrow; he understands how you feel. Furthermore, God can use you to console others in the future with the same comfort He provided you in this time of grief (2 Corinthians 1:3-7).

God's comfort is such that He will never let you face a challenge you can't manage. He constantly provides a road for healing (1 Corinthians 10:13). One of His favourite ways to help us cope with tragedy is to encourage us to console others. It's also important to remember that God has a purpose for you even in the middle of your loss and pain. He adores you and promises to help you heal. And if you believe Him, He will give you the grace to rebuild your life (Jer 31:3-4).

Even when no one else will, God is willing to console you, support you, and hold your hand during terrible times. But first, He seeks your permission to do all of this. God will not force his way into your heart.You may be bearing a lot of burdens. Maybe you're exhausted and unable to move forward. Christ's invitation is, "Come unto me, all ye that labour and are heavy laden, and I will give you rest." (Matthew 11:28).

Christ Gives Us Hope

In describing the goal of His ministry, Jesus quoted this text found in the Old Testament: *"The Spirit of the Lord God is upon me; because the Lord hath anointed me to preach good tidings unto the meek; he hath sent me to bind up the brokenhearted, to proclaim liberty to the captives, and the opening of the prison to them that are bound; To proclaim the acceptable year of the Lord, and the day of vengeance of our God; to comfort all that mourn; To appoint unto them that mourn in Zion, to give unto them beauty for ashes, the oil of joy for mourning, the garment of praise for the spirit of heaviness; that they might be called trees of righteousness, the planting of the Lord, that he might be glorified."* (Isaiah 61:1-3).

In addition to liberating and rescuing people from the consequences of sin, Christ consoled those in sorrow. Be encouraged; God provides comfort! Consider the terms highlighted in bold as you read the poem above. This is the work of God. He is now willing and eager to work in your life through His Spirit to heal, comfort, and console. This reveals that Jesus came to restore His people and give them abundant life (John 10:10).

Furthermore, Christ's healing ministry on Earth did not conclude with His ascension to heaven. Instead, He pledged to never leave or forsake His children (Hebrews 13:5). His presence will always be with us through the Holy Spirit. *"If ye had known me, ye should have known my Father also: and from henceforth ye know him, and have seen him."* (John 14:7). Furthermore, Christ's healing ministry on Earth did not end when He ascended to heaven. Instead, He promised to never leave or abandon His children (Hebrews 13:5). His presence will always be with us through the Holy Spirit. The word "helper" in Greek means "comforter." When Jesus ascended to heaven, He sent the Holy Spirit to continue His mission on Earth. Jesus guarantees us peace via the Holy Spirit's activities. God's presence in our life can be sensed through the Holy Spirit.

Why This Good News?

Because the Bible states that we might find much-needed joy in His presence (Psalm 16:11). When we focus our minds on God, He offers us complete peace (Isaiah 26:3). And it is via the Holy Spirit that we can always be in God's presence and keep our attention fixed on Him. As a result, you can be confident that God will be with you through any storms that life may bring your way. He promises to support you through the pain of loss and grieving. And He offers you peace that surpasses all human understanding (Philippians 4:7).

How Does God Respond to Those Who Grieve?

Job's struggle with grieving is one of the most well-known stories in the Bible. Job was a committed disciple of God who interacted with Him on a daily basis. One day, Satan contacted God and told Him that Job only served Him because of all the benefits He bestowed upon him. So God put Job to the test. The test was designed to evaluate if Job's trust was based on what God had given him or on who God is a relational, loving God. So God allowed Satan to take away everything He had given Job but his life (Job 1). In a matter of seconds, Job had lost his donkeys, oxen, lambs, camels, servants, and even his children. It's difficult to imagine how he must have felt. How did he react? He got up, took off his clothing, and shaved his head. These were his culture's strategies for expressing profound sadness and mourning. He then does something else. Job falls to the ground and worships God, saying: *"And said, Naked came I out of my mother's womb, and naked shall I return thither: the Lord gave, and the Lord hath taken away; blessed be the name of the Lord."* We are told that *"in all this Job did not sin nor charge God with wrong"* (Job 1:21,22).

Job had such a close relationship with his Creator that he trusted that anything God chose to do with His life would work out well in the end. During his ordeal, his close friends abandoned him (Job 19:14-15). Even his wife exclaimed at one point, *"Dost thou still retain thine integrity?" "Curse God and die."* Unfortunately, many people continue to have similar experiences today. You may have had a moment of loss during when the individuals closest to you seemed the most distant. Others might have turned against you. You, like Job, may have wondered why God was silent (30:20).

Job had a lot of questions at the time. He didn't understand why things happened the way they did. He must've wondered where God was when he needed Him. But God breaks the silence in Job 38-42. He asks Job questions he can't answer. Questions that even academics cannot claim to understand. God reveals Himself as the infinite God. The one who knows the outcome from the beginning. It's important mentioning that God doesn't get offended when we ask questions. He is a reasonable God, and He enjoys discussing things with us. When we want to communicate with our Creator. That's why He says, *"Come now, and let us reason together, saith the Lord: though your sins be as scarlet, they shall be as white as snow; though they be red like crimson, they shall be as wool."* Isaiah 1:18. He encourages questioning, but we must finally believe that He is in control. He works for the salvation of everyone who believe in Him, and He has your best interests in mind.

God's existence, character, laws, and plans are priceless. Nonetheless, He wants to gradually train us to have faith in Him. We place our situation in God's sympathetic, powerful hands. He offers ample evidence of His compassion to us, His earthly descendants, so that we might have faith in Him. He asks us all the same question: *"Will you trust Me even when life takes an unexpected turn?"* Job's experience shows that God is aware of all events. God sees everything, from life's most serious problems to the smallest tears, and He hears our hearts' prayers.

No matter what problem comes our way, God promises to eventually turn it all around and make it all *"And we know that all things work together for good to them that love God, to those who are called according to His purpose."* (Rom. 8:28). Though God allowed Job to face difficult hardships, this was not God's initial plan. We must never forget that we are in the midst of a tremendous dispute. We live in a world that knows both "good and evil" (Genesis 3:5, 22) as a result of humanity's decisions. However, Satan is the one who strives to destroy and inflict suffering for all of us. And his efforts to bend and deform our world might be overwhelming at times. He is cruel and evil, and he enjoys manipulating your emotions. Then he will attempt to persuade everyone that God is the source of the world's immense misery, pain, and grief. As you can see, this is a discussion over God's character. In many ways, we can all relate to Job. We could also try to respond like Job did, always seeking comfort from the Lord, trusting in His goodness, and clinging to His gentle hand even throughout the most difficult trials.

Jesus Christ

Jesus Christ is a wonderful illustration of sadness. The Bible calls Him a "man of sorrows" who was/is "acquainted with grief" (Isaiah 53:3). Throughout His life, Jesus had a personal connection with people who had experienced loss, suffering, despair, and the pain of death. He was constantly worried about those in need and strove to ease their pain. Nonetheless, He experienced considerably greater grief than His disciples or those to whom He ministered.

Jesus was killed for our sins (1 Peter 2:24). The creator's hands were nailed on the cross for us. For those He lovingly made and gave life to. And He endured the agony of complete separation from God on our behalf.Those who convicted him insulted, spat on, assaulted, whipped, and treated him as a slave. All the while, He was dying for them. He went through all of this so that each and every one of us could be reconciled with God and have eternal life.Isn't this sobering? Then His disciples left him (Mark 14:50). His own countrymen had abandoned him (John 1:11). Nonetheless, He bore all humanity's sin, whether or not they accepted His offer of salvation for their lives (Isaiah 53:6).

When Christ was crucified, He cried out under the weight of sin: "And in the ninth hour, Jesus yelled with a loud voice, crying, Eli, Eli, lama sabachthani? "My God, why have you abandoned me?" (See Matthew 27:46). Jesus' experience was intense. He bore the world's sins, was abandoned by His people, and cried out to God because He couldn't feel His Father's love. Despite this, he remained focused on the others. He also prayed for those who crucified Him: "Father, forgive them" (Luke 23:34). In tremendous anguish, He asked His lover John to look after His mother (John 19:25–27). Another example of selfless devotion. reads, "But God commendeth his love towards us, in that, while we were yet sinners, Christ died for us." Romans 5:8.

Christ endured all of this for the sake of others, no himself. Jesus died because God loved him and desired to save fallen humanity. God loves us in an eternal way (Jeremiah 31:3. He proved this in concrete terms via Christ's experience of sorrow and suffering on the Cross. "I love you" is a beautiful sentence that we appreciate hearing between two people. But how much more beautiful and profound is it when God communicates personally to us?

The Father's heart was wrenched during Christ's agony on the cross, when He was abandoned because of the sin He carried. The sun did not shine, thus the place was gloomy (Luke 23:44–45). How awful it must have been for God to see His Son die! However, it was in that pitch-black darkness, with Jesus hanging on the cross. *"Christ hath redeemed us from the curse of the law, being made a curse for us: for it is written, Cursed is every one that hangeth on a tree:"* (Galatians 3:13).

The seemingly hopeless condition of Christ's death heralds a day when pain, suffering, loss, sin, death, and tears shall all vanish (Revelation 21:4). Thus, the Bible exhorts us *"Looking unto Jesus the author and finisher of our faith; who for the joy that was set before him endured the cross, despising the shame, and is set down at the right hand of the throne of God."* Hebrews 12:2.

Christ's experience with grief teaches us three things:

- Christ understands our suffering; in fact, He experienced far more suffering than we could have imagined.

- In the midst of misery and suffering, Christ worked to relieve the pain of others.

- God's heart breaks when He sees His earthly children's agony, but it is His goal to restore harmony: "And we know that all things work together for good to them that love God, to those who are called according to his purpose."

Let us consider a well-known psalm that emphasises this concept: *"Yea, though I walk through the valley of the shadow of death, I will fear no evil: for thou art with me; thy rod and thy staff they comfort me."* Psalm 23:4. Christ is our shepherd, guiding us through the valley of the shadow of death. The path may appear dark and murky at times, but with Him as our leader, we have grace for the journey and hope for better pastures at the end.

God's Assurances To Those Who Grieve

Here are some promises from God's word that you might pray about. Tell God about your experiences, your pain, and your sadness; claim these promises and believe that God will keep them.

- *"Blessed are they that mourn: for they shall be comforted."* (Matthew verse 4).

- *"My flesh and my heart faileth: but God is the strength of my heart, and my portion for ever."* (Psalm 73:26, emphasis added)

- *"Jesus said unto her, I am the resurrection, and the life: he that believeth in me, though he were dead, yet shall he live:' And whosoever liveth and believeth in me shall never die. Believest thou this?"* (John 11:25, 26).

- *"The Lord is nigh unto them that are of a broken heart; and saveth such as be of a contrite spirit."* (Psalm 34:18)

- *"He healeth the broken in heart, and bindeth up their wounds."* (Psalm 147:3).

- *"Let not your heart be troubled: ye believe in God, believe also in me. In my Father's house are many mansions: if it were not so, I would have told you. I go to prepare a place for you. And if I go and prepare a place for you, I will come again, and receive you unto myself; that where I am, there ye may be also." (John 14:1-3).*

- *"And we know that all things work together for good to them that love God, to them who are the called according to his purpose."* (Romans 8:28).

- *"For the Lord himself shall descend from heaven with a shout, with the voice of the archangel, and with the trump of God: and the dead in Christ shall rise first:"* (1 Thessalonians 4:16).

- *"Peace I leave with you, my peace I give unto you: not as the world giveth, give I unto you. Let not your heart be troubled, neither let it be afraid."* (John 14:27)

- *"Fear thou not; for I am with thee: be not dismayed; for I am thy God: I will strengthen thee; yea, I will help thee; yea, I will uphold thee with the right hand of my righteousness."* (Isaiah 41:10).

-

Hope for Those Who Remain Faithful to Christ

Even though Satan is doomed to fail, there is still a genuine battle for the salvation of our souls. Jesus wants us to remember that He has the keys to the grave (Revelation 1:17-18), and that His death on the cross defeated Satan and, eventually, death itself (1 Corinthians 15:51-54). The truth is that sin has soiled the earth, and Satan knows that his time is running out.

And thus, for the time we have left on earth, God wants you to *"set your affection on things above, not on things on earth."* Colossians 3:2. We are to keep looking ahead, because there is hope beyond our current situation! The Bible directs us to a time of hope, in which, *"And God shall wipe away all tears from their eyes; and there shall be no more death, sorrow, crying, nor pain: for the former things have passed away."* This scripture is extremely encouraging to those of us who are grieving! Jesus gladly endured the cross and profound grief for each of us. He is aware of the anguish you have encountered in your life, and He extends His hand and invites you to walk with Him through the consoling ministry of the Holy Spirit.

Despite the anguish, He found joy in knowing that He would be with you and your loved ones for eternity. And when we cling to God's promises in difficult circumstances, let our minds be on Christ, the joy of our salvation. May we, like Jesus, try to relieve others by sharing the comfort we have received from God. And soon, He will return and take us home, out of this world of sin and pain. Hallelujah, that is our blessed hope!

In Conclusion

As we've shown in this article, the dead have no consciousness; they know and feel nothing. People who die do not go to heaven or hell, but rather continue to exist in consciousness. They proceed to the grave, where their bodies disintegrate because the life force has been withdrawn. They are sleeping, completely unaware of what is happening on Earth or in Heaven. The Bible plainly states that the good dead are not in heaven, and the wicked dead are not in a region of burning. They are in the dust of the earth, awaiting the resurrection day. That day, for the virtuous, will mark Christ's second coming. For the wicked, it will be at the end of the millennium, when they will be roused for judgement and cast into eternal sleep.

About the Author

I learned about the Bible in the Religious Instruction classes in my freshman year of secondary school. But in a different class with the same professor, we discussed evolution, and I saw then that a degree in theology is no guarantee of a person's genuine Christian faith or adherence to biblical values.

The symbolic themes in Daniel and Revelation didn't make sense to me until I read Ellen G. White's 'The Great Controversy' a long time after I had already researched a lot of different religions. Presently, I document my knowledge thus far in the form of little books. In reading this book, I hope you may gain some useful information.